Tuk-tuks, Whiteboards, and Sticky Rice

Tales from Beyond the Mekong

Daniel Whetham

Sarah
GRACE
PUBLISHING

First published 2022 by Malcolm Down Publishing Ltd
www.malcolmdown.co.uk

25 24 23 22   7 6 5 4 3 2 1

British Library Cataloguing in Publication Data
A catalogue record for this book is available from the British Library.

ISBN 978-1-915046-28-4

Cover Illustration by Keziah Whetham
Cover design by Esther Kotecha
Art direction by Sarah Grace
Photos by Daniel Whetham

Printed in the UK

Contents

Endorsements

Join Daniel and Mei and their family as they negotiate the life of a young couple living overseas. The vivid account of their adventures, the sights and sounds of Laos – the food, the smells, the mosquitoes – jump out of every page. But the story is more than that. It is the story of the faithfulness of God in providing for and directing them, and the story of their walk of faith as they find their feet, pursue their mission, and trust in God in every circumstance. Highly recommended!

Richard Harvey, All Nations Christian College, England

A personal, vivid and engaging narrative for any aspiring cross-cultural worker who wants down-to-earth insights of living and serving in Laos or the Mekong region! The authenticity and over-a-decade experience of the author and his family make this book a must-read for especially cross-cultural missional families who want to understand what incarnational mission looks like in a foreign land.

Christy Lim, National Director, Interserve Singapore

Right from the very first moment I met with Daniel and Mei over lunch in a bustling Singapore street, their love and passion for the peoples of South East Asia was so apparent. Theirs was not an easy journey, but the call on their lives to serve God in this part of the world was strong. It was the country of Laos that captured their hearts, and they went on to serve there for twelve years. During that time, they impacted many lives, both the people of Laos they served with such willing hearts and the colleagues they worked alongside.

This will be a must-read for anyone contemplating service in South East Asia. Thank you, Daniel and Mei (and their two lovely daughters, Keziah and Kaelyn), for all that you have contributed during your time in Laos.

Ken Martin, Regional Director for their sending agency

What a pleasure to read *Tuk-Tuks, Whiteboards and Sticky Rice* by Daniel Whetham. He has written a very helpful book for those who are seeking their calling to serve cross-culturally, as well as people who are caring for mission workers. Daniel's candid and vivid writing adds authenticity as well as a personal touch on issues such as discerning one's calling, language learning, cross-cultural adaptation and contextualisation. Daily interactions with people of different backgrounds (both Lao and expats), encounters with creatures big and small (cats, snakes, scorpions, cockroaches, etc.), regular battles with negativity, and the Spirit's working through unexpected turns of events – provide a colourful and rich, albeit real, depiction of the life of a cross-culture, bi-vocational minister. I resonate with the insightful reflections which serve as a catalyst towards mission awareness, and I highly recommend this book to anyone seeking to advance the Great Commission.

Revd Chua Yeow San, Senior Pastor of Grace Singapore Chinese Christian Church

Daniel has taken me, through this delightful book, on a journey to one of the most beautiful countries and peoples in the world. He writes in an engaging way that I believe will draw his readers in, as he describes life and ministry in Laos. The language, culture, food, lifestyle, people, climate, transport, and stories about ministry and family life – all described in ways that bring daily life, in a country so different from our own, truly alive. At times I caught myself laughing out loud and at other times I shed tears as I read.

The Whetham family's clear sense of God's call on their lives and their subsequent obedience to that call, took them into places and situations that would have been beyond their imaginations before they got on that plane and stepped out in faith. What an example to all who would follow God's lead.

Daniel's dedication, not just to God's call to go to Laos, but also his dedication to God's call on him to teach, shines through. His passion for teaching and his desire to see his students thrive in every sense of the word is both admirable and inspirational. His willingness to recall mistakes and failures as well as successes make the whole story believable and alive. His ability to laugh at himself and some of the situations the family found themselves in is honest and refreshing.

I would recommend this book to anyone who is interested in cross-cultural mission, whether in going or in supporting those who go. It gives valuable insights into the joys and struggles, alongside teaching tips and advice for anyone living in South East Asia, particularly Laos. It will help you to know how to pray for those who serve cross culturally. And maybe for some, God will use this beautifully written book to call you to go. I pray that if that happens, you will obey, and as you serve Him to reach others with His love (as Daniel, Mei, Keziah and Kaelyn have done) you will be blessed.

Jane Fucella, former mission partner on the Thai/Lao border. Previously Chair of Interserve International Council

A hot-off-the-aeroplane memoir from a passionate missionary to Laos. Daniel writes poignantly for his two daughters, that they might have some insight into 'the things that were going on in the lives and heads of your parents as we tried to make sense of living in Laos as a family'. This family clearly loved Laos: its people, pace of life, animals, and beauty. They clearly fitted in well there, spending twelve happy years serving the Lao people through friendship, fellowship, English Language teaching, and simply sharing life together. Not that Daniel papers over the cracks – you'll read about termites turning everything to dust, drug-crazed neighbours, near-lethal journeys, sweaty heat, noise pollution, murdered cats, visa frustration, and oppressive religious darkness, but through it all shines their gospel optimism.

A highlight for me was the culturally sensitive, carefully considered section on reaching Buddhist people using English teaching in authentic and loving ways, without either coercing them or attacking their existing beliefs. People came to Christ – not everybody, but those the Lord was seeking. But if you're more interested in fauna than faith, keep your eyes open for the lesser-known Asian unicorn! A really helpful read for anybody going into mission in South East Asia, especially families, but also anyone wanting to use English teaching for outreach; in whichever part of the globe they find themselves.

David Baldwin, Global Missions Director, Oak Hill College, London

From the Author

Dear Keziah and Kaelyn,

You loved living in Laos with your friends and collection of pets of all shapes and sizes. One of our favourite things is thinking back with you and discussing our sad, funny, and unusual experiences of Laos. Some of your lovely drawings of Laos are included in this book.

I have written down these memories so that one day when you feel curious enough, you may have some insight into some of the things that were going on in the lives and heads of your parents as we tried to make sense of living in Laos as a family.

Love, Dad

For readers of this book,

I hope that as you read these experiences, you will get a sense of how Laos has a mysterious way of getting deep under your skin. Our sending organisation uses the motto, 'People for the hard places', but Mei and I never felt that way about Laos. Even with its trials and heartaches, we learned to deeply appreciate the beauty and grace of the land and its people. The extra resilience, resources, time, and effort demanded of those who seek to walk alongside the people of Laos is well worth the cost.

Although we pledged from the start to 'give the best of our years' to Laos, we received so much in return. It is unbelievable in some ways that we are at this milestone of gathering stories from twelve years in the country. I am very thankful to Mei for her love and support over the years and help in recalling many of our experiences. This book is an invitation to join our family as we do battle with insistent insects, scratch our heads over furry friends, lie awake at night mulling over schooling and visa 'options', and navigate the challenges and joys of walking alongside local people in the stunning country we call 'home'.

Twelve Years in Laos: A Timeline (2008–2020) and Map

Map of Laos by Keziah Whetham

July 2008 – December 2008 (Vientiane)

Intensive language learning and orientation to the English Centre where Daniel taught under our business visas. A time of blossoming relationship 'for life' with local and expat people alike.

January 2009 – December 2009 (Pakse)

We moved from Vientiane to our 'long-term placement' at a branch of the English Centre in Pakse, a thirteen-hour bus journey to the south. What a time of joy with two other families with small children who had also just joined the Centre. Mei home-schooled Keziah alongside other children and also helped Lao teenagers who were training to become house-helpers. Along with the other husbands, Daniel launched into a full-load of English classes. Connections were built with students, many of whom we still stay in touch with.

It was not long before we heard rumblings of a dispute among the leaders at the English Centre. Although we were not involved, the atmosphere was unsettling. As we poured out our hearts to a visiting friend, she prayed that all the people involved would be removed. Was this kind of gritty, irreverent, pain-filled demand even allowed? Imagine our utter shock when it was spectacularly answered. The English Centre as we knew it had come to an end.

Although gut-wrenching, we were no longer bound to the situation. With tears, we headed to the UK on 'Home Assignment'. Little did we realise how God had plans to work something good out of the pain we had experienced. The ripples, however, of how Christians acted in 2009 can still be felt today.

June 2010 – May 2017 (Vientiane)

We felt God leading us back to the English Centre we had started out with in Vientiane. We found joy getting stuck into the local and expat fellowships. We grasped the opportunity of working on our Lao language. In 2011, our longed-for second daughter, Kaelyn, was born.

Shortly afterwards, our mouths literally fell open when we were asked to manage the English Centre in Vientiane. We had been harbouring a desire to return to the provinces but God was showing us a different way. Teaching in the capital city would enable fantastic opportunities to meet the many people who had come in from the provinces.

The English Centre needed teachers but they did not stay all that long. We set about creating a positive work culture at the Centre that people wanted to be a part of. We felt God asking us to focus on connecting with the poor, those in government, and the monks in the temples. Our hearts were full as God nudged teachers from around the world to come and teach, and who stayed longer.

Our office was abuzz with local and expat staff eager to share about their lives. We listened, gave advice, assisted, and prayed for countless people with many breakthroughs. Although negativity and gossip reared their ugly heads once in a while, a community was being built. In wonder, we recount all the opportunities to witness and be blessed within our homes, at the Centre, and in the villages.

June 2017 – August 2020 (Savannakhet)

What joy to return to the provinces after so many years in the capital. Friends from Vientiane travelled with us and helped get our home ready. At the English Centre, we found ourselves in the role of 'go-between' among the expat and local staff, helping with linguistic and cultural communication. We were no longer in leadership and it was sometimes hard not to be able to take action when people and the Centre struggled. God, however, continued to encourage us as people committed their lives to Him.

We were knocked for six, however, when we felt God calling us to England. Daniel's mother had become unwell. Teachers were increasingly hard to come by at Keziah's school and we needed to see her through the GCSE and A-level years. Although heart-broken at leaving, we felt Him encouraging us that all our years in Laos were precious and not in vain. He would continue to be with us through this next season of our lives.

Chapter 1 – Entering a Black Hole

The grey water of the snaking Mekong swirled below as the plane swooped low over vast, flooded plains of fluorescent paddy fields. As aircraft tyres thudded safely onto cement, we realised with relief and joy that we had arrived.

It was 2008 when my wife, Mei (pronounced like the month), our daughter, Keziah, and I, first arrived on Lao soil. It still feels fresh as if it was yesterday. We were thirty-one and twenty-nine years old. Our daughter was two. A British man, a Singaporean lady, and a toddler, stepping out from the familiar and the comfortable into the unknown.

Finally, we were embarking upon the adventure we felt so strongly the Lord was ushering us into. We took Habakkuk 3:19 as our encouragement and leaned on Him for the stamina and agility of a deer on 'high places'. It only dawned on us later what a terrible privilege it was to be released by family and friends into His care. After we had left for Laos, my mother said it was if we had disappeared into a black hole.

Sabaidee and Hello. We invite you to read just a selection of experiences and recollections from twelve years of working, living, and being a family in Laos, also known officially as the Lao People's Democratic Republic or Lao PDR.[1]

So right off the bat, allow me to clarify something. A question we often get asked is whether the country is 'Laos' or 'Lao'. As a language teacher, you will need to bear with me. There are no words in the Lao language with a final 's' (not counting words borrowed from other languages). It was the former French colonial masters who coined 'Laos', adding

---

1. Laos is also sometimes referred to as *Lan Xang*, the land of a million elephants. Around 1353, Fa Ngum declared the kingdom of *Lan Xang Hom Kao* (a million elephants under a white parasol), symbols that spoke of power and authority (see Grant Evans, *A Short History of Laos: The Land In Between*, Australia: Allen & Unwin, 2002, p10).

the 's' because of the dominant Lao people group. As 'Laos' has stuck internationally, we tend to use it when talking in English, while 'Lao' is more like an adjective (e.g. Lao food). When we are interacting in the Lao language, however, the country is always 'Lao', including *Pathet Lao* or *Muang Lao* (the country and nation of Laos).

We often get asked how we met and ended up in Laos, a little-known country far from the minds of most people. From an early age, we had been captivated by Jesus. We had accepted the life to the full Jesus was offering with an identity rooted in Him. As we allowed our lives to be surrendered to Him, we experienced deep satisfaction and contentment. On top of that, we had sensed a special 'calling' on our lives – a divine instinct, guidance, motivation if you will – to be prepared and poised, in order to answer His call to go to 'other places' to be witnesses to Him: His light, His life.

From an early age, I wanted to be a teacher to much teasing from my peers who were going to be doctors and engineers! I wanted to make a difference in needy situations and in the lives of children. Little did I know that, over the years, I would adapt and grow in my understanding of teaching as 'access' or 'a way in' to difficult situations, a visa in order to live in a country otherwise unwelcoming to foreigners, a job parallel but not necessarily integrated into life as a whole. Surely teaching enabled all these things and yet pondering how the actual teaching itself could be witness to Him was also a huge part of the process.

After trudging doggedly through studies in education, I felt drawn to the urgent needs of crowded, multicultural London. I soon found myself in a gritty, urban primary school with children from all over the world and the travelling community. The situation was needy to say the least. Teachers were in short supply. Classes were bursting at the seams. The Victorian-era rooms were small with children joining late and squeezing in. Many had special needs, behavioural issues, and tragic, difficult home lives.

I had to find a way of keeping a class of thirty-three on track, plus preparation and marking, not to mention coping with stressed-out colleagues. What a task to make sense of it all and keep a hold of my faith, starting each day with a deep breath and stepping out with forgiveness, hope, and love. I learned how to stay very calm amidst turmoil which would be very useful in unpredictable Laos! Although relishing living in the heart of London and learning a lot about teaching, there was a persistent stirring in my heart to step into serving Him through teaching overseas.

Going to Laos was never a stretch as Asia held a certain fascination for me. Moreover, I was brought up in South Asia by parents serving God there. When my parents moved the family to England, they specifically chose to continue their witness by living in the midst of one of the largest South Asian communities in the UK. Living 'alongside' in the heart of communities with all its challenges and joys made an incredible impression. Not giving up on people but gently persevering in gentleness, prayer, and compassion were hallmarks of my parents' outreach and witness.

When a Christian organisation shared a pressing need for a primary teacher in Nepal for the children of development workers, my ears pricked up. Asia beckoned; the need was urgent. They needed someone like me. Just like that, I eagerly accepted. The one-year post was voluntary although I had some meagre savings. I would be the only teacher and would teach the twelve children as a group although they ranged from six to twelve years old.

When my parents coordinated a sending-off for me, to my astonishment they placed a bucket in the middle of the room. I suddenly realised what it was for. It was incredibly moving to experience God's care through the love and generosity of people who provided just about enough to see me through the next year. Little would I know that God would ask my wife and I to live out this pattern time and time again, that is, trusting by faith that finances would be provided. Although the provision often looked unlikely, the exact amount we needed would come in and often at the eleventh hour.

After a straightforward connecting flight to Kathmandu via the Middle East, the person supposed to be picking me up from the airport did not turn up! I was in a strange country in a throng of people. My head buzzed, I felt dizzy, and it was hard to remain calm amidst the clamour. After what seemed like an age, someone from the organisation whose kids I would be teaching eventually arrived with endless apologies and a tiny, green car. Breathing a sigh of relief, I was whisked away through the crowds to my accommodation.

I found myself in Kathmandu's twin city of Patan or Lalitpur, so near the zoo I could hear the roar of the animals. Every morning, I would clamber up a makeshift ladder to the flat roof to ponder and pray in the relative calm away from the bustling streets. Distant snow-capped mountains adorned the horizon. This habit of getting away from daily concerns and noise became so important over the years, in order to be still, receive, and hear from Father God.

I loved working with the children who were from all over the world but, all too quickly, my teaching contract in Nepal ended. A TESOL[2] course in England awaited which I hoped would broaden my teaching skills and open up more opportunities to serve Him. Before returning to England, I travelled by train from Chiang Rai in northern Thailand to Singapore, stopping off to visit friends and projects connected with Nepal along the way.

It was in Singapore that I met Mei at a mission conference and we instantly connected with our desire to use our teaching backgrounds for God in Asia. We were unsure about the where and how but we knew

---

2. There are a confusing number of acronyms with very similar meanings including Teaching English to Speakers of Other Languages (TESOL), Teaching English as a Foreign Language (TEFL), and Teaching English as a Second Language (TESL).

this is what we wanted to do with our lives. We needed to get to know each other more, however, and we came from countries so different and so far from one another. We prayed that if He led me to a TESOL job in Singapore, we would take it as a sign that we should pursue the relationship. This was the beginning of a journey together that would see us placing our very lives in the Father's hands time and time again.

Before leaving for England, I enquired with a well-known English Language Centre near frenetic Orchard Road as to whether they needed teachers in the future. It seemed unlikely. I was not even trained in TESOL yet. The amazing thing was that the director was not only available but willing to meet me. After buying me a coffee and patiently listening to my story, she shared how the English Centre valued primary teachers because of their experience in managing classroom setups and knowledge of how children and young people learn. I held my breath as she said she was willing to take a chance on me if I could be back in Singapore in five months. It was all rather miraculous yet only a verbal agreement.

On returning to England in August 2002, there was no written confirmation of a job offer from the English Centre and by October our plans were looking as bleak as the freezing, relentless rain. Just as we were about to give up, the email I had been waiting for finally arrived with a job offer to start in January. A one-way ticket to Singapore could finally be booked.

Mei's pathway to serving Him in Laos held many more challenges. She grew up in a non-Christian family with her parents following a form of Buddhism that involved veneration of the ancestors. After accepting God in her life through the witness of a teacher in the Girls' Brigade, how could she face the agonising situation of honouring her parents despite their opposition to her faith? The awful feeling of being alone, particularly in an Asian culture that valued togetherness, did not last for long, however, as her older sister had also become a Christian.

As her parents gradually accepted their daughter's new commitment to Jesus as Lord, Mei decided to work for a Christian organisation in Singapore and studied how to teach English to children through 'Speech and Drama'. This kickstarted her love for teaching and the interaction it gave with people. Several short-term trips to Thailand and Indonesia with her church helped seal her determination to serve Him in South East Asia for the longer term. Laos never crossed her mind!

The idea of their daughter marrying a foreigner did not exactly thrill Mei's parents and they asked half in jest whether there were not any Chinese men left in Singapore. I sadly never met Mei's father as he passed away suddenly with leukaemia. Mei's mum welcomed me as part of the family and I soon learned all sorts of practical Chinese expressions. We can say with joy that definitely one of the most astonishing answers to many years of persevering in prayer was Mei's mother coming to faith.

Being part of a highly competitive and successful financial powerhouse, Singaporeans, like a lot of people, consider education, career, and economic security as non-negotiable priorities. A few weeks or a month or two for the kind of overseas work we wanted to do was acceptable. For Mei to commit to a place such as Laos for the long-term was mindboggling and unacceptable for many folks. We were throwing away our education and careers, not to mention safety, stability, and opportunities for our children. I have particular respect for the Singaporeans I meet who have taken the courageous step of faith of going overseas to serve Him, amidst the incredibly powerful pressures that financial incentives exert.

It was quite astonishing how many folks assumed that Mei and the girls were based in Singapore with myself living in Laos. Perhaps this kind of fragmented 'commuter' ministry was an option among what many saw as the non-negotiables of education and job accessibility. We were so proud of Mei's mother whenever she reminded people that not only were we committed to Laos but were content there. Over the years, we found that satisfaction was a powerful witness to the God who not only calls but equips and provides.[3]

When we decided to get engaged, Mei and I realised we needed grounding in cross-cultural work. We had it all worked out. After enrolling on a year's course at All Nations Christian College[4] in the south of England, we would get married during the Easter holidays. The wedding would be in Singapore followed by a blessing service in England for all the people who could not travel so far away.

Our one-year course morphed into three. We were shaken when my father suddenly passed away just before our wedding. He was only 64. How had God allowed this to happen? Then in 2006, just over a year and a half later, we received the gift of our precious first child, Keziah. Psalm 147:3 describes the tenderness of a God who sees and binds our wounds. The joy and delight of a new marriage and child were intermingled with turmoil, heartache, depression, and exhaustion.

Laos had not crossed our minds during our studies. Rather, papers were submitted in the context of Myanmar, discussing Buddhism and folk religion, the pros and cons of orphanage care, and the ethics of using English teaching as a means to evangelism. In our final year, we really appreciated the on-site crèche for baby Keziah during the mornings. At night, however, we soon discovered that she would only drop off curled up tight against one of us. Which was fine until the final dissertations when I somehow found a way of typing up my all-night final paper one-handed with Keziah snoozing contentedly on my lap.

---

3. We found satisfaction from experiencing God Himself, along with His care and provision (see Isaiah 55:1-3). Nevertheless, He also provided the things we needed (like Moses in Exodus 4) and equipped us with good things to do His will (Hebrews 13:20-21).

4. https://allnations.ac.uk/ (accessed 21 February, 2022).

The one small sticking point with our plans for Myanmar was that our sending organisation did not have placements there for English teachers. Then in 2007, the Myanmar government started tinkering with fuel subsidies resulting in a 'saffron uprising' with monks leading popular demonstrations against the authorities. This led to a military crackdown and amidst the ensuing chaos, injuries, and loss of life, we were dismayed but not surprised that our organisation would not be pursuing a placement there for us.

Things were looking really disappointing when a colleague from our organisation got in touch and eagerly related how he had just returned from scoping out potential partnerships in Asia. A newly-opened Christian-led English Centre in the south of Laos needed English teachers. It is not a simple thing to explain 'calling' in everyday terms but the opportunity rang true, an urgent need that we could assist with, a magnetism towards a country, a people, a context. The path we were to follow was placed before us. As we stepped out in faith, the deep peace we experienced was comforting and supernatural.[5] People often tried to clarify how long we had in mind but there was never any time frame. We had pledged the best of our years.

Once we had graduated from All Nations, we moved to my parents' house in Oldham, a large industrial town in Manchester. We needed to begin the task of building prayer and financial support among family, friends, and church groups for the work we believed we had been called to in Laos. From a human perspective, this was an uphill battle. We lived in an impoverished area with lots of unemployment and social problems. Moreover, many people were from other religious backgrounds. This part of England was not known for its large, healthy church communities.

---

5. There were many things to be afraid of and nervous about. 'The Unknown' was one of them. These God-given emotions were not to be denied but His presence and peace allowed us to act with courage and faith (see John 14:27).

Nevertheless, as we prayed and asked Father God to meet our needs, our daily bread if you will, it was humbling to experience the interest for our family and the task in Laos. One small church that we had been attending was popular with international people and asylum seekers who had settled in the area. We were astonished when the church leaders invited us to head up their youth programme together with finances towards our support raising.

What an experience guiding a boisterous bunch of Ugandan and Nigerian teens through 'Youth Alpha',[6] an introductory course to the Christian faith. Our last session together discussed the Spirit and many of the teens took the opportunity of asking Him into their lives. It was a powerful and emotional time. We still keep in touch today.

The church organised a wonderful commissioning service to send us off to Laos, with friends attending from all the churches that we had been involved with over the years. Friends even jetted in from Northern Ireland and a former tutor from All Nations came all the way to Oldham to stand with us.

Before heading to Laos, the plan was to first go to Singapore to spend some time with Mei's family. We had experienced His goodness through the generosity of friends, family, and local churches, but we were still below our support target. Understandably, the policy of our sending organisation was to only release people overseas when funds were sufficient.

Humanly speaking, we had exhausted our contacts and we could not ask any more of the local churches, many of whom were struggling themselves. God had other plans though and nudged me to contact the English Centre in Singapore where I had taught previously. Could I do

---

6. It was essential to adapt resources to make them relevant for the people involved (see https://alpha.org/youth/ accessed 21 February, 2022).

some work for them for a few months to bring our support levels up to target?

It was a long shot but amazingly, they were keen to have me back. After a nerve-racking telephone interview, I was offered a job with enough flexibility and time in-between to seek support among Singaporean churches while looking after my young family. Once again, at the last minute in our rollercoaster faith journey, God provided. Bags could now be packed for the long flight to Singapore.

With the motivation of bolstering our support levels for Laos, our time in Singapore went quickly. We took every opportunity of spending time with family, visiting churches, and taking our toddler, Keziah, to all the family-friendly sites the city-state is so famous for.

After a few weeks of working at the English Centre, I plucked up the courage to tell the manager some of my story. Her withering response was not exactly encouraging. My heart skipped a beat as she told me in no uncertain terms what she thought of Christians! The miraculous thing was she then told me about her sister who had decided to go to Cambodia where she was working with the church. The thing was that even with very real misgivings, her heart had been softened. The next thing I knew, all sorts of teaching projects were mysteriously channelled my way which boosted our fundraising no end.

It was a fulfilling time working with people from all over the world teaching English in branches across Singapore to children as young as six right up to adult learners, while also editing and expanding curriculum for young learners. The English Centre tried to tempt me in all sorts of lucrative ways to extend my contract. However, the way before us was clear and we resolved not to be swayed by finances but to stay faithful and walk in it.

I remember writing to many Singapore churches asking about their involvement in overseas work and potential interest for our work in Laos. I only received one reply. It was hard not to feel discouraged. Although Mei was from Singapore, it was hard for people to understand who we were and the work we wanted to do. Clearly, Laos was not on the radar of most people, even those committed to sharing the good news about Jesus far and wide. Perhaps it was our job to help more people know about Laos and the needs there.

Once again, He was working in the details although we could only trust in His provision by faith. We needed to step out without seeing the full picture, with or without financial backing. We did not know that even after we had arrived on Lao soil, some very tentative links with two churches in Singapore were miraculously taking seed, progressively growing over the years, and eventually blossoming in stunning colour. Little did we see in those early years how the long-term care and support of these groups of people for us would be a phenomenal, beautiful thing.

Our time in Singapore was drawing to a close and we needed to start preparing to head to Laos. Learning the Lao language was our top priority because we wanted to communicate with people in their heart language as soon as possible. However, our sending organisation and the English Centre in Laos advised us that finding a trained teacher of Lao in the south of Laos would be nearly impossible. We needed to first head to the Lao capital of Vientiane (pronounced 'Vien-chan'), where there were trained, local teachers.

We would also receive some orientation from colleagues in our sending organisation and the English Centre ('Never ride a motorbike without a helmet!', 'Always lock your teaching cupboard!'). After a couple of months, I would teach a reduced load of six hours a week of English classes until December. Then, after settling down nicely, we would uproot to Pakse in January and the English teaching would increase to twelve hours a week.

The idea of shipping belongings from Singapore into Laos in 2008 had never occurred to us and, in any case, we were determined to live simply without distractions. There were no plans to come out of Laos again for the foreseeable future. Even so, it was encouraging when a contact from a church in Singapore connected in with the airlines offered us free extra baggage allowance. This meant some more things could be packed that would almost certainly not be available in Laos, especially for our toddler.

Imagine our shock when, a few days before travel, we received a call explaining that the baggage was actually for donations of clothing for the needy in Laos. Mei had already packed up to the limit. However, after explaining that this was our first journey to live in Laos long-term with a small child, the misunderstanding was cleared up and just like that, the extra allowance was again ours to use.

With support-raising still borderline, we had planned to travel a day before Keziah turned two which saved money on an infant's fare compared to a child's ticket. A few days before travel, however, Keziah and I fell ill and we resigned ourselves to postponing the travel date and paying the higher child fare. While Keziah soon got better, the antibiotics did not make any difference for my ear infection. My head throbbed, I could not stand for long because of the dizziness. Friends dropped by to pray and counsel that we should again postpone.

I would be the first not to recommend anyone travelling unwell when moving for the first time to another country. After so much waiting and preparation, however, I could not bear any more delay. The adrenaline and focus pushed aside the nausea and light-headedness.

Our adventure together in Laos had begun, spearheading a new chapter in our lives that would last twelve years. When we disembarked from the aircraft at Wattay Airport in Vientiane, it was like being hosed down with hot air. The terminal was tranquil and calm. The lift down to baggage reclaim was broken. As Mei waited for her visa at passport control, I set down our toddler at the foot of the stairs with strict instructions not to move while I ran up and down three times to retrieve our infinite carry-on items.

Once out of the airport, it was a relief to be met by a colleague from the English Centre. Soon afterwards, we found ourselves standing near the English Centre alongside a six-lane cement road divided by a concrete barrier full of rumbling traffic. Not quite the image of stilt houses nestling in the sunset by a sleepy, meandering river.

A mass of pickups, small goods trucks, *tuk-tuks*,[7] and motorbikes hurtled past sending up clouds of dust and pollution, a noticeable lack of helmets throughout. We would soon discover that donning a helmet in such sweltering heat not only diminished hearing but left your head drenched in perspiration and spoiled your hairstyle. Choosing to wear one, however, greatly increased your chances of survival in an accident. Not wearing one was the surest way to being fined by the police. Nevertheles, we saw that a lot of people kept their helmets in the front basket of their motorbikes, only putting them on when nearing checkpoints on the main roads.

As we surveyed the passing blur of humanity, it was clear that Laos did not prevent its women from getting out and about. Even quite a few of the men wore their hair long. Apart from all the people driving vehicles, it was notable how hardly anyone seemed to be around, walking or cycling. Perhaps this was not all that startling considering the oppressive humidity and fierce glare of the sun. How were we supposed to meet people let alone connect with them? The heart-breaking thing was that many of the people we did see in the heat of the day were begging or mentally unstable. No one seemed to notice them. No one at all.

---

7. Small, spluttering, colourful, three-wheeled vehicles, really just a motorbike drawing a covered platform with two rows to sit on.

The English Centre had helpfully arranged for us to stay at the on-site guestroom for a couple of weeks until our rental accommodation became available. We quickly realised that we would be getting to sleep late because of the thumping bass continuing until two in the morning from the nightclub at the nearby prestigious hotel. When we mentioned our woes to a colleague, she was indignant as officially Lao nightclubs were supposed to wind down much earlier. To our shock, she immediately went to have a word with the hotel management. Perhaps it was our imagination but for a few days afterwards, the music seemed to be ever so slightly softer and stopped a bit earlier.

The guestroom was upstairs next to a staffroom for teachers and other offices, an area which was secured at night once the door at the top of the stairs was locked, from the inside. One evening, after devotedly bolting the door and settling down to an early night, we jumped up in astonishment at the tremendous shouting and battering coming from outside. Having just turned up in Laos, our imaginations ran riot. Perhaps an argument had got out of hand? Were we being evicted or even arrested? Maybe thieves or a drunken mob were demanding entrance?

Upon extremely cautious investigation, the door was gingerly unbolted, and an irate teacher was discovered standing outside. He had conspired to finish teaching a little later than normal and found himself locked out with his bag and car keys still inside the staffroom.

On our first proper day in Laos, we were hungry so I ventured out in the searing heat to the main road to try and find something edible. Mei and Keziah were not all that enthralled by the two miniscule, bony, fried fish I had managed to procure from what seemed like the only food stall for miles. Wrapped in banana leaves, the fish came with two plastic bags filled with *khao niao* (sticky rice) and *padek*, the pungent, dark brown, fermented fish sauce loved by all Lao. One friend would show us later how it was made by wrapping fish in banana leaves and hanging them in the hot sun for three days!

In the evenings, as the sun was beginning to set, we would saunter into the city centre with Keziah in her pushchair, complete with a battery-operated pink miniature fan. She enthralled everyone we passed and people insisted on trying out the fan on themselves. Each day, we would sample the different food options ranging from humble family-run establishments jutting out precariously onto the swirling waters of the Mekong ('No *padek* please!') to homely French-Lao eateries with cosy wooden balconies.

We were starting to make some sort of sense of the Black Hole. What a privilege to have arrived in Laos. We had been given a welcoming and safe place at the English Centre from which to explore. It was time to get to know people but first we needed to move into our own house and learn how to speak the local language.

Chapter 2 – All Creatures Great and Small

How glad we were to move into our rental house, although it was in the middle of the rainy season. It was what the Lao rather grandly called a *villa*, a single-storey bungalow with two bedrooms. It was perfect for our small family. Although the lush, tropical garden was submerged underwater with the heavy rain, we were delighted with the wildly cascading *dok jia* (the lovely 'paper flower' or bougainvillaea) all over the perimeter walls.

We were still in the UK when we were alerted by a leader at the English Centre that the house would soon be up for rent. Renting a house unseen was a real step of faith! However, we only needed something for five months before moving to our long-term placement in Pakse, thirteen hours away in the south. We did not own a vehicle and the house was within walking distance from the English Centre. Moreover, the landlord had a good reputation and was willing to do six months rather than the customary year's rental.

A month's deposit needed to be paid on our behalf by the English Centre to secure the house. Understandably, the leader at the English Centre was quite anxious that we would not change our minds. We would later discover that others had disliked accommodation that had been paid in advance for them and declined to take care of the costs. All at a cost to relationships. Little did we know that in the years to come, we would also find ourselves with a similar 'heavy' responsibility of finding safe, affordable, and comfortable accommodation for the many teachers we encouraged to come and serve in Laos.

The landlord of our house was the first Lao person we met outside the English Centre. What a positive first impression of the people we longed to understand and build relationships with. Jovial and concerned for our well-being, he insisted that we turned on all the lights inside and out at night to discourage would-be thieves.

When it became impossible to walk around the side of the house without sinking ankle-deep in rain-soaked sludge, he immediately set to work on an artistic, crazy-paving pathway across the grass. He was more of a father-figure really, popping over early every Sunday morning with a deafening petrol-powered lawnmower. What a unique motivation for getting up early to escape the noise and walk up the road to the local church.

The lovely bougainvillea of Laos amongst the tropical undergrowth

The houses that we saw in the urban centres were invariably made from a combination of brick, cement, and copious amounts of wood, raised off the ground to prevent floodwater entering. Screened windows kept the incessant mosquitoes at bay. The daytime-biting potentially dengue-carrying *aedes* variety had black and white legs while the dawn-to-dusk *anopheles* ones of malaria infamy landed in a higher position. I must confess to not giving much thought to checking these fascinating facts before rapidly dispatching whatever was biting me.

The diseases mosquitoes brought with them were very real. We did not want to take long-term medication as the side-effects were worrying. Without running air-conditioning non-stop, sleeping under mosquito nets was far too stuffy. Instead, the many holes in the ageing window screens were covered with tape, doors were kept closed, light traps and sprays were deployed, and fans constantly whirred to blow the insects off-course.

Our very favourite tool against mosquitoes were rechargeable racquets with an electric charge along the bars in the middle. They were great fun and good exercise as you swished to and fro wherever mosquitoes were buzzing around. Which was pretty much everywhere. It was just like playing tennis. Even if you looked ever-so-slightly ridiculous. There was an unequalled sense of satisfaction when a loud crackling indicated there was one less mosquito in the world.

It did not take us long to befriend our inquisitive and friendly neighbours. One young girl plucked up courage to tell Mei how everyone next door watched with fascination as I religiously swished my racquet over our shoes outside the front door each morning.

Endless zapping entertainment was assured by rustling curtains, hung-up laundry, and motorbike helmets. Everyone in Laos had at least one of these essentials and we knew people who even brought them back to the UK for the midges. Picture this: the often stern-looking officials at the border were forever swishing their racquets around under the tables and chairs where the mosquitoes had a field-day feeding on their heels. They loved it when I asked in Lao if they were enjoying their game of tennis.

We soon discovered that the vacant space underneath the roof was reserved for members of the animal kingdom to congregate, particularly at night. Imagine huddling inside your sheet with your light-sleeping two-year old, listening to the disjointed symphony of snarling neighbourhood cats, coupled with the deafening roar of rampant nightly monsoon rain. Picture the sweet relief as the downpour finally ceases, the animal kingdom above rests at last, and your weary head sinks down again. Only to be woken by hundreds of frogs and toads offering heart-felt croaks from just outside your bedroom window.

The Bible verses reassuring us that the Lord gave sleep to those He loved was not exactly encouraging during these sorts of experiences.[8] With increasing sleep-deprived desperation, I recall googling how to discourage frogs. The only workable answer was to place plastic snakes all over the garden. As finding toy shops, let alone plastic snakes, was a near-impossible task in Laos in 2008, we had to grin and bear it. Nowadays, whenever we see toy snakes for sale, we think of those frogs sent to improve our characters in Laos.

One particular night, long after we had gone to sleep, we heard a dreadful splintering sound erupt from the ceiling and bolted from our beds to investigate. Picture a gaping hole in the ceiling at one o'clock in the morning along with a rather bewildered cat sprawled in the middle of scattered debris. It had somehow avoided the whirring ceiling fan. The befuddled moggie was promptly shown the door while we wearily hammered a nail or two to secure the fragile ceiling boards back to their rightful place.

Whenever we talked to the local people about unwanted animals wandering about, it became clear that Buddhist temples were the answer. They were seen as dumping grounds for animals, especially cats, due to the Buddhist belief in preserving life (and not 'interfering' with

---

8. Sleep deprivation did eat into morale and the ability to remember God's presence and care (see Psalm 127:2).

life by neutering). In Buddhist thinking, the life of an animal was to be respected because it could be a person reincarnated. As Buddhist beliefs meant that no meat was to be consumed, temples were one place we saw cats gustily eating sticky rice! If they were lucky, more nourishment could be gained from the scraps on the floor from the eateries that surrounded the safe haven of the temples.

We were dismayed at just how many people, including foreigners, simply passed on the issue of constantly-breeding cats to the temples without a second thought. This overwhelmed the monks and resulted in a lot of hungry, sickly, and suffering animals wandering about, often to be attacked by dogs or run over by the swarm of passing cars and motorbikes.

We felt 'called' to Laos but we desperately wanted our children to feel part of the adventure God had given us. Having pets helped our family have a sense of connection and 'home'. When our daughter, Keziah, longed for a kitten, I took her to visit our local temple. At the back of my mind, I wanted to make some connections with the monks and see if they were interested in learning English. I also wanted to help with the burden of looking after all these unwanted animals. Immediately on arrival, a beaming novice monk in his orange robes smiled and asked in Lao how he could be of assistance. When I enquired if there were by any chance any kittens around, he cheerfully replied, 'Yes, how many do you want?'

Somehow, we always ended up with cats as pets. Signs on many gates warned passers-by in Lao to 'Beware of the fierce dog' in ominous, dripping, blood-red script. How our local friends rolled around laughing when we asked about making a 'Beware of the fierce cat' sign for our house.

In addition, one of our local friends insisted on giving us a couple of chicks and we kept them in a wooden enclosure in the garden. Early one morning, Mei sensed something moving around in the undergrowth outside the house. On inspection, I discovered that an aggressive dog belonging to the neighbour had squeezed in under the gate, smashed through the chicken run, and killed all the chicks.

On extracting the frenzied dog with a large stick, I stupidly got too close and suffered a worrying, nasty bite to my finger which called for a prompt rabies check. I knew it was unwise to act upon emotions in Laos and especially to act alone. Nevertheless, with thumping heart, I gathered up the dead chicks and marched with still-bleeding finger to the pearly gates adorning the mansion of the neighbour whose dog it was.

After an age, a tiny window opened a crack in the gate and I tried to calmly explain my case in my best Lao to the man of the house inside. I was trembling. The window slammed shut without reply and I was left standing in the rain. The rudeness was astonishing. I wondered whether that was the end of it. After what seemed like an age, a child pushed a thousand Thai *baht* note (about £20 at the time) through the window before it rapidly clanked shut again. No apology and comment except in the form of money which did not cover the checks at the clinic. I got an inkling of how the powerless feel when forced to plead an injustice. Lord, do not forget the helpless![9] Despondent and soaked through, I was left to trudge back home and explain things to two shocked and upset children.

Not long afterwards, the children were shocked to see our cat sprawled on the porch, covered with blood, apparently clipped by a passing motorbike. It was late in the day and the only available people who could help were two energetic French vets. They duly informed me that their specialism was elephants! The amputation on slightly smaller bones was a success and our three-legged cat lived out a decent life, still managing to climb to the tree tops.

---

9. The Psalms are full of honest, heartfelt cries for God to act in response to unjust situations and people (e.g. Psalm 10:12,14).

Perhaps we owe our very lives to our cat friends. An incident seared into our minds happened while the children were playing in the garden. Our gormless but faithful cat went all tense in attack mode. It was then that I spotted a large snake curled up metres away from the children, head high scrutinising our cat which was fearlessly and naïvely skulking up on it. Shouting to Mei for a spade, I threw a bucket at the cat which reluctantly scampered off. When I spun around to finish off the snake with the spade, it had vanished. With horror and gratefulness, I noted that it had been in exactly the path the children would have run along back to the house.

The children ran the same way to their favourite swing every day

I would often chance upon snakes burrowed in the drains and pipes leading to and from the house. Always switch the lights on before stepping into the bathroom. Always peer into the toilet bowl before use! We were indebted to our brave cats for the variety of mangled snake corpses regularly deposited on the cement outside. When we found two mangled scorpions under our washing machine, we realised they must have come off second-best to our cats at some point and scuttled away to expire. In the semi-darkness of that room, we could have easily agitated one in our flip-flops.

Knocking out our shoes and sandals before putting them on was essential in case some horrid creature had fled inside. One monster we kept a constant eye-out for was the fiery-red Lao centipede, a quick, ferocious fighter which packed a venomous bite requiring hospital treatment. Mostly, however, a harmless cloud of mosquitoes would fly out or a pompous-looking toad would peer out and hop away.

There were few things more annoying than incessant buzzing from mosquitoes trapped in your motorbike helmet. Leaving work one day, I devotedly put on my motorbike helmet before getting on my trusty bike for the twenty-minute slog across town. Aware of a hysterical mosquito buzzing around inside my helmet, I made haste to remove it on reaching home. A black palm-sized spider clambered out and scuttled away. Always shake out your helmet and shoes before use!

To keep mosquitoes down, we tolerated the many kinds of lizards in and around our house. However, it was one of the worst feelings in the world to step on one with your bare feet or have one fall on your head or even down your t-shirt as you walked past. We were forever wiping up the little white and black souvenirs deposited along the windowsills and the girls were fascinated by the tiny, translucent egg balls ingeniously secreted behind books, toys, and plants.

I always feel guilty about the time I popped round to see a Lao friend and spotted his cat in a tree, all strange and tense on a low-lying branch. It did not even look at me when I called its name. A group of animated men suddenly bustled out of the door from some sort of meeting and followed my gaze to the cat. On a branch just above it, a huge lizard perched precariously, eyes bulging. With a cry of excitement, one of the men slowly advanced and deftly caught the ill-fated creature by its neck. Dinner was provided!

Being a vegetarian was not always easy in Laos. I remember being invited to eat with friends in their village. My mother accompanied us and told us afterwards about the eye that popped up in her soup and stared at her. On another occasion, being completely loyal to everything Lao, Mei and I thought we would go to a famous local restaurant. We just could not bring ourselves to finish our servings of fried crickets, grilled frog, and pig intestines, to name a few delights.

Another time, I was visiting friends in a village when the host suddenly thought it would be great sport to capture and kill a pig using a net weighed down with rocks. Luckily for the frenzied animal and my nerves, the throws were woefully inaccurate and I managed to find an appropriate excuse to exit before things progressed.

Courtesy of Mei being Singaporean, we enjoyed our links to the Embassy. Once we were even invited to lunch with the Ambassador! After an hour or so chatting about teaching English and life in the south of Laos, we headed to the English Centre to prep for our evening classes. While chatting to the staff, I noticed the neighbour's two dogs zealously sniffing around the tyres of our car parked outside. Nothing unusual there! However, anticipating that their next move would be to raise a leg, I rushed out to shoo them away.

As we got in the car to return home, I thought it prudent to first check the engine to make sure nothing was there. Clicking open the bonnet revealed one rather harassed-looking cat sitting on the battery. Having suffered nasty gashes on my hands the last time I dared to rescue two wide-eyed, innocent-looking strays from our car engine, I shooed this one out and away. It leapt right into the main road with a motorbike swerving just in time to avoid it. Now the neighbour's dogs were on to it in a frenzy and the cat ran zigzag back across the road and into a Vietnamese restaurant packed with people standing around and hollering out their orders. A Vietnamese restaurant is never a good place for any animal!

It was at this point Kaelyn shouted out that she reckoned it was actually our cat. I chased the cat in and among the people waiting for food. No one batted an eyelid. The barmy foreigner was at it again. No news there. The cat slipped through some fencing on the side and down a narrow alleyway separating the adjoining houses. I clambered down the alley pushing aside giant cobwebs and closing large wooden window shutters while calling out whether anyone was home. Luckily no one seemed to be around as my very foreign-looking six-foot frame would have almost certainly caused a heart attack to anyone investigating. The alley eventually came to a dead end and there, hiding under a protruding plant, was one extremely traumatised cat. Our cat. It had survived two car journeys in a whirring engine, sat for more than an hour inside a piping hot contraption, escaped two ferocious dogs, and dodged a speeding motorbike.

One of our favourite things in Laos was the plentiful, luscious tropical fruit. In no time, our Lao friends got us hooked on the marvellous ritual of *gin som* (literally 'eating sour'). Unripe green mangoes provided the sour taste and a blend of salt, sugar, chilli powder, and MSG[10] provided the dip. We wholeheartedly agree with the veteran worker who declared that to survive long-term in Laos you had to *gin som* every day. This was a great insight as it was very hard to eat this snack alone. Within

---

10. Monosodium glutamate, the flavour-enhancing, thirst-inducing food additive used in all Lao cooking. We suspected it contributed to some side-effects in our children such as hyper-activity.

minutes, folks would gather to dip and catch up on the latest news.

Little did we know that mango trees always came with strings attached. We were always security-conscious to the amusement of our friends, putting away gadgets, closing windows, locking cupboards and doors, and securing the outside gate whenever we left the house.

The front gates we saw in Laos were often worthy of heaven, a chance to display perceived wealth with ornate metalwork in gaudy colours. The goal was both security and prestige and the whole point was being able to peer through the bars. The negative side was that it was easy to see at a glance if someone was in or out, especially if there was a padlock on the outside of the door or the gate.

One trick we employed was slipping our hands through the bars of the gate and locking the padlock on the inside. It took some practice, especially if, like me, you had large hands and clumsy fingers. The idea was that it made it look as if someone was home and put doubt in the mind of anyone up to any mischief. At least we liked to think so. This was all very well until you accidentally dropped your keys on the inside of the locked gate and spent the next fifteen minutes trying to poke them back out with a stick.

On returning home one evening, we reached through the bars of the gate to unlock the padlock inside. Instantly, we found our hands, arms, and neck covered with enraged red fighting ants, each one applying a bite resulting in an angry red welt, followed by mad scratching.

What we had not realised was that the branches of our mango tree had provided a most convenient bridge to the gate for the insect world. Any locals watching would have clutched their sides in laughter at the sight of two foreigners wildly dancing around and throwing their arms and bodies around in a bid to get rid of the creatures. Those fighting ants made for the most effective house security and all for free. Even if they were not able to distinguish between the rightful occupants. Over the years, we adored the fruit for the taking in our various gardens but begrudgingly acknowledged and respected the guardians of the mango trees.

'Glorious mango fruit' by Keziah Whetham

Another of our closest friends over the years were wood termites. They trailed us wherever we laid our hats. We paid little attention at first to the wiggling, cream-coloured maggots poking their heads out of the wooden surfaces. The little piles of dust on the door and window frames, and even tiles were mildly distracting but, to be honest, there was dust everywhere.

After spending two months away in the UK, we returned to our home and upon opening a cupboard, discovered that its entire contents had dissolved into a pile of dust, including not only the chipboard shelving, but clothes, a sleeping bag, and even a camera and its battery. Somewhere there were luminous yellow termites ravenously seeking something else to devour. Friends encouraged us to keep the leftover remnants of wood and paper as the twisting and turning of the little gobblers had resulted in intricate patterns and shapes worthy of an art exhibition. We turned down this opportunity and made a huge bonfire instead.

More seriously, we discovered that termites had weakened wood panelling in the ceiling at the English Centre after a large rotating ceiling fan crashed down in the middle of a church meeting, narrowly missing a feeding mother at the back. Crucially, the wiring of the fan in the ceiling slowed its descent which averted certain tragedy.

Shares in termite spray must have rocketed during our time in Laos as we contributed a small fortune over the years by smothering wooden surfaces with foul, throat-burning insecticide. Add slash-and-burn agriculture, burning of plastic, and vehicle pollution (not a few vehicles run without catalytic converters), and we had an inkling as to why both Keziah and myself suffered from chronic bronchitis over the years.

Termites did not occupy the minds of our local friends at all. Once hatched into flying insects, they made a convenient and nutritious snack. Meanwhile, we continued to find termites in trees leaning ominously over the house, the heavy solid wood frames of our bed, curtains, and the supporting wooden beams of the roof. Whenever we ate outside, we often had to turn the lights off and eat in darkness otherwise thousands of flying ants would descend into our hair, clothes, and bowls of food. Not one of our local friends ever batted an eyelid at this most mundane of occurrences.

We often lived near unofficial cockfighting rings which would invariably spring up at the weekend, all with much raucous laughter and shouting. On more than one occasion, a clever bird that knew I was the only vegetarian for miles would break for freedom into our garden. On eventual capture, the owner would tuck it under his arm, stroke it, and talk to it like a child. Only for the same thing to happen all over again a few days later.

Once a small cockerel wandered into our garden and adopted Keziah. It ran to her whenever she called it, sat on her lap, and gazed lovingly at her. It always made Kaelyn cry as it insisted on depositing a special something on her toys. Over time, we became fonder of its eccentricities, marvelling how it jostled the cats for the fish and chicken bones and even once ran across the garden with a boiled egg in its beak.

A rooster finds refuge in our garden

Animals not only kept us company over the years but protected us. Our Lao friends could see our care for creation by our gentle approach to animals. Animals also enabled us to connect with people whether friends at school, our neighbours, or the monks in the temples. They

43

were a great reason to practise our Lao. The array of animals and insects in our lives over our years in Laos, whether by choice or not, certainly brought a lot of joy and not a few headaches into our lives. Together with some great memories, all the experiences probably had something to do with my distinct lack of hair.

Chapter 3 – Navigating from A to B

Basking in the refreshing breeze of the night, I cycled along, the darkness of the road hardly illuminated by the sporadic lampposts. With a sudden jolt, my bicycle suddenly crashed to a stop, catapulting me over the handlebars with instant pain as skin met with cement. A yelp and a shape slinking into the shadows confirmed I had just cycled right into a dog!

The accident must have worked something loose on the bicycle, as the entire contraption literally just came apart on my next slog to work. Again, I ended up sprawled in a heap on the side of the road. No one else was around at all. There was little choice but to lock various bits of bicycle to an electricity pylon and scurry to work on foot, dripping with exertion and smothered in filthy bicycle grease. Needless to say, the bicycle was rapidly donated to our Lao neighbours who managed to fix it up in no time for their children to play with.

Although the English Centre was only a short walk away, the stifling heat and humidity meant that movement needed to be accomplished gradually and gracefully, an art all local people have mastered. Lugging along a backpack with laptop and teaching books in formal clothing without arriving at work thoroughly soaked was a near-impossible task. Our Lao colleagues and students, meanwhile, always managed to arrive looking flawless with barely a single bead of moisture on their foreheads.

Learning Lao was the priority and Mei managed to arrange for a sought-after Lao teacher to teach her at home. This was ideal since she needed to keep an eye on Keziah who was toddling around and watching cartoons. Our teacher helped us to start speaking Lao in no time and also invited us to our first local church experience. We hummed along to the lively music and singing with keyboard, drums, and electric guitars. We were surprised but grateful for the air conditioning and whirring overhead fans. Everyone sat on heavy wooden pews in rows: women on the left, men on the right. Everyone faced forwards.

I decided to learn Lao in a group at a reputable language centre. The only snag was that it was right on the other side of town. How could I get there for 9am with no recognisable public transport system to speak of and no vehicle of our own or to borrow? Waiting for a *tuk-tuk*, shared fixed-route *sawntaeo*,[11] or a *jumbo*[12] was the only way. First, I needed to cross six lanes of chaotic traffic which required nerves of steel and the dexterity of an antelope. When a colleague said it was easier to drive from her house to the English Centre rather than cross this particular road, I thought she was being a bit dramatic. Until it was my turn.

Endless streams of motorbikes and trucks shot past but with a bit of patience a *tuk-tuk* usually rumbled up eventually. The linguistic adventure began as I enquired as to the destination, repeated this at least three times for mutual comprehension, used amateur dramatics (fingers to count, smiles, devastated facial expressions), and numbers just learned in class to bring down the asking price. I would then cram my six-foot frame onto the rumbling podium filled to the brim with people, rice sacks, and livestock before hurtling into traffic.

On arrival at the language centre, there was just enough time to grab a 'Thai tea' from a roadside stall, a heart-pumping concoction of fluorescent orange instant tea powder swirled together with condensed milk, syrup, ice, and little black 'pearls' of tapioca all sucked up through an oversized straw. An absolute essential for the upcoming brutal three hours of speaking and reading.

The Lao teachers were admirably trained not to use or even respond to English throughout the lessons and patiently coaxed forth impossible sounds such as '*ng*' at the start of words. One teacher was particularly

---

11. Literally 'two rows' (of seats), I preferred these vehicles simply because they were roomier, faster, and quieter than tuk-tuks.
12. A large flat-bed small goods or pick-up truck with higher roof and two rows of seats.

stern and students cowered under her withering '*Bor*' ('No') to most things we contributed. Naturally, her homework tasks were always completed without fail and I learned much quicker than I would have done in a more lenient situation with English to fall back on.

Language-learning was hard-going. Whenever it was my turn to answer, there would be sighs, chuckles, or drumming of fingers from a fellow student who had studied some Thai already, a language quite similar to Lao. However, my solitary moment of triumph was coming. I learned that there were more consonant sounds in Lao than English with 't' and 'd', for example, having softer versions that sound like 'dt' and 'th'. For some unfathomable reason, I not only could hear the difference between such consonants but articulated them, much to the astonishment of my classmates and applause of the teachers. My success with the Lao language more or less ended there.

Along the long tramp back home after each class, I would find myself reading the shop signs in Lao, laboriously sounding out letter-by-letter combinations to make words, the meanings often elusive. One day, I literally jumped for joy after reading out one word from a sign, recognising its meaning, checking with the English that happened to be underneath, and finding out I was correct. Any onlookers would have been forgiven for thinking what an odd species this foreigner was for suddenly leaping about in the middle of the road.

Walking was one way to quickly get to know people and shops in the neighbourhood. The boisterous, friendly *bing gai* (grilled chicken) lady at the end of the road. The jovial, welcoming family selling fiery *tam mak hung* (papaya salad) from the front of their shack. The outgoing former monk with excellent English running the local minimart with the raucous pre-school upstairs.

When walking by a group of people eating, chances were that they called out, *'Ma gin khao'* (literally, 'Come and eat rice'). For the Lao, it was certainly an odd thing to eat alone. Lao friends often remarked that if you ate alone, the food would not be *sep* (delicious).

This orientation to inclusivity, sharing, and generosity made for a lovely approach to life and we soon found ourselves calling out to friends and strangers alike to *ma gin khao*. There was no obligation, however, to stop and devour other people's food. The polite refusal, *Seun sep* ('May it be delicious', literally an 'invitation to deliciousness'), we were taught in language class certainly resulted in a few hearty laughs. Perhaps it was over-polite or simply sounded bizarre coming from foreigners. A smile and a word or two would often suffice before moving on.

We loved the way 'Come and eat!' acknowledged the presence of others and the importance of food in togetherness and community. *Ma gin khao* acted as a greeting, an apology almost, that you were busy engaging in an activity that excluded but now invited people to come and partake.

It was amazing how food enabled opportunities to connect with people whom we had little in common with or even a shared language. The eating experience itself was designed with community in mind. The Lao are the world's great sticky rice eaters. The interesting thing was how the rice only stuck to itself. The rice would be held in a rattan basket, often a piece of woven artwork in itself. The basket would be handed around for everyone to grab a fistful of rice. Small balls of rice were then rolled in the hand to dip into nearby communal spicy sauces and soups. Food, as a matter of local etiquette, was duly divided up amongst everyone present. Whether fried chicken or fish on a stick, pungent bamboo shoot soup, or pickled vegetables in a plastic bag, all would receive their portion.

'Sticky rice in a basket' by Keziah Whetham

When we were invited to eat at someone's house, we had to get used to not expecting the food to be served soon after arrival. No, our arrival signalled when the food would start to be prepared, cooked, or even caught. By everyone together. All of this communicated how relationships were more important than tasks and time. People often said that Lao PDR was short for 'Please don't rush'. Slowing down and savouring people and places certainly became an addictive and healthy approach to life.

Another 'question' people would often call out was, *"Pai sai?"* ('Where are you going?' or literally, 'Go where?'). At first, we would try and explain until it soon became clear this too was another greeting, similar to 'How are you?', which recognised and engaged but did not expect a detailed reply. We soon got the hang of smiling and calling back, 'Out', 'Over there', or 'Shopping' as we passed neighbours. These simple opportunities at interaction would have been impossible if we were whizzing around on a motorbike or in a car.

With this in mind, we would recommend intentionally holding back on securing a vehicle for at least the first few weeks. Walking did become overrated, however, when you needed to get to a meeting or teach in formal attire across town in the searing heat. Having a motorbike gave the deep satisfaction of knowing that in the city, you would get to your destination before any car as you weaved in and out of traffic. Until it started raining, a tyre went flat, the police stopped you, or you got caught up in an accident.

Friends were generous to lend us motorbikes and we held off for six months before deciding to purchase our own. It was actually put off for longer when my wallet containing the money for the motorbike mysteriously went missing on the way to the motorbike shop. I did get a phone call three months later from someone trying to sell me back my wallet minus the cash.

In the meantime, a police report was required to make some sort of insurance claim. In hindsight, I went with jaw-dropping over-confidence to the police station by myself. After outlining my predicament in basic Lao, it became clear after an hour or so of waiting that the stern-looking policeman wanted me to wait further while his colleagues responded to his radio call. My teaching hours were gradually approaching and he was not at all pleased when I explained that I would soon have to leave for work. I was told in no uncertain terms to stay where I was. I was the one being detained now. When I could not wait any longer, I caused him to lose face big-time by excusing myself and rushing out of the door.

As a good Christian, it is time to confess that after this experience, I thought it simpler to type up an official-looking insurance report myself with translation from an obliging colleague at the English Centre. You will be glad to hear that it was the genuine, official stamp of the village headman, however, that graced the foot of the letter. A few weeks later, however, who would turn up at our gate looking worse the wear for drink but the very same policeman who had detained me. It had not taken much detective work as hardly any foreigners lived in town. We were nervous that he had come to cause trouble.

We sat him down in our living room and served tea and snacks and were relieved to discover that he had come to enquire about learning English. His goal in life was to get a posting at the Lao-Thai border where income would be much more forthcoming. For that he needed English and my help. He promised that he would drink lots of beer before class to help him talk. We were rather thankful that after a few more conversations, he gave up calling and did not visit again.

When a bright red 115cc Korean-Lao motorbike was eventually purchased, our friends were amazed how it ran for nearly three weeks on the moonshine put in by the shop on day one. After that, I could never completely trust the fuel gauge and the contraption would sometimes splutter to a standstill with no gas to run on. I was giving a rather portly friend a lift across the city when my bike did exactly this. Luckily, I managed to roll down a steep hill in neutral to a roadside stall with glass bottles of watered-down fuel for sale at exorbitant prices. With a whisper, I was also informed by the stallholder that drugs were available should I be interested.

Another time on the way to work, the bike suddenly ran out of fuel and stopped in the middle of one of the busiest roads in the city. Luckily, I was heading downhill and trundled along in neutral on the edge of the road. I noted with increasing dismay that every gas station seemed to have run out of fuel. An arduous, sweaty walk pushing my motorbike to the office was the subsequent result.

Turning the wrong way on a motorbike down a one-way alley was easy to do in the narrow, twisting lanes of Lao cities. One day, I started to turn right but on seeing the no-right-turn sign at the last minute, I swerved my motorbike around before entering. A group of waiting policemen immediately waved me over. Quite understandably, they believed that I had every intention of hurtling down the road and only turned back after seeing them.

A fine for the traffic violation was in order. The prevailing local perspective was that if I was not in the country in the first place, this would never have happened. No arguing with that logic. I thought I was being clever and kind by offering to buy them all noodle soup instead. Suddenly, a large group of policemen came round the corner and my original fine suddenly became a whole lot more.

It was really quite unusual to see anyone walking anywhere much further than the next block. Lao dogs knew this. Many dogs we met in Laos were domesticated, calm, loving, pampered pooches. With one difference: they were often allowed – no, encouraged – to roam out of the confines of the household to which they belonged. This was ingenious as cleaning up any mess was out of sight, out of mind.

This meant, however, that anyone odd enough to be sauntering along the street was sure to be greeted by an enormous racket and sometimes worse if a dog or three rushed up to you. Many people carried around a handful of pebbles as it was frightening to be faced with aggressive animals, especially with rabies and other nasty diseases about. A favourite trick was stooping down as if to pick up a stone, causing most dogs to get the message and skulk off without further ado.

Something about bicycles and motorbikes seemed to drive many of the dogs crazy as they would run right up and alongside while nipping at your heels. After the initial shock, you quickly found yourself perfecting the art of keeping a moving motorbike upwards while kicking out at the errant animal, all in such a graceful manner that no one even looked up to see what all the noise was about.

In desperation, I even invested in a dog-training device that emitted a high frequency whine that dogs apparently could not stand. Very useful for warding off the dogs that barked non-stop right outside our bedroom window at night. It was even loaned to a colleague who had to walk past several aggressive dogs on her way to work. She returned it a few months later reporting that they now totally avoided her!

With any mode of transportation, vigilant driving at all times was in order. Even some of the flashy vehicles seemed to have a broken rear light or two which meant the person in front could suddenly slow down, turn, or even stop without warning. Leaving a generous stopping distance between the next vehicle and yourself was advisable although such good intentions would be dashed as the space instantly filled with motorbikes. With overtaking on the inside a constant possibility, blind spots needed to be continually scrutinised. Indicators needed to be switched on well before turning.

Even while parked, I could not let my guard down. When opening my car door a crack, I instantly struck a glancing blow to a passing motorbike. In a split second, the rider somersaulted spectacularly over the handlebars, landing on the rough of the cement road. The bike slid to a halt nearby. Miraculously, he was unharmed except for grazed hands. Thanking God, apologising, and cross with him for riding so incredibly close to the parked cars, I pressed some money into his hand for the repair of his motorbike which was remarkably unscathed except for an oil rupture. The dent at the bottom of my car door served as a constant reminder to be vigilant.

Thankfully, traffic was never that fast or aggressive and the truly remarkable thing was that hardly anyone used their horn. We tried to find the reason behind this with no real satisfactory answer. One explanation from a local friend was that the Lao are extremely sensitive about unnecessarily shocking another person and causing their protective spirits to come out from them. Regrettably, this perspective did not extend to karaoke, phones, and loudspeakers.

The replacement for honking your horn in Laos seemed to be flashing your lights. This was never used for giving way. Flashing your lights essentially communicated that, 'I'm here and coming through!' The only problem was when two or more vehicles flashed their lights at the same time. Then things rapidly became interesting with a game of chicken ensuing and usually the bigger vehicle begrudgingly given preference. Perhaps this was the Lao equivalent of road-rage with a lot of unnecessarily close calls and accidents.

One way of causing instant pandemonium was by attempting to give way or letting a poor soul cross the road by stopping, smiling, and waving your hand. I got some very odd looks, shakes of the head, and bemused smiles at such eccentricity. Just flash your lights and pile on through.

At roundabouts, the vehicle that was in the circle first had the right of way. This 'rule' was backed up by informative little signs. In reality, vehicle size and light-flashing still made all the difference as everyone charged forward to get inside the circle first. This inevitably led to infuriating and hilarious roundabout traffic jams with everyone locked inside the circle until someone ultimately gave up and gave way.

Becoming accustomed to driving Lao-style happened amazingly quickly. It became so natural and common-sense that when I attempted similar manoeuvres in my passport country, I found it hard to fathom all the honks, choice words, and angry looks thrown my way.

With thieves rampant, our local friends pleaded with us to follow their example by hauling their bikes inside at night. Most Lao homes were set off the ground and reached by two or three steps as a precaution against rising water in the wet season. A sloping block of wood or cement was used to drag motorbikes up and inside. After devotedly following this security method for a couple of days, we realised that a large, dirty, smelly, and piping-hot machine in the middle of our living room did not really contribute towards the lovely home we had always dreamed of.

The final straw came when one evening, while dragging my motorbike into the house, I conspired to scrape the stand across my big toe. My big toe nail was torn right off in the process. Agony! From then on, the motorbike was consigned to a tiny outside toilet room. The time taken to wiggle and angle that motorbike to and fro into the tiny gap between the wall and toilet bowl was staggering but beat having to drag it in and out of the house every single day.

Another precaution against theft was to purchase a D-lock, handily stored on the frame of the front wheel. Little did we know that after a few weeks of bouncing about on the uneven roads, it had steadily been working itself loose. On arriving home one day, I was shocked to see the lock nearly hanging off. The thing was that a few more minutes of travel would have seen it careering into the spokes causing a catastrophic head-over-heels accident even at low speed. At first, Mei did not grasp what I was saying as we had just installed the lock at some expense. However, as it dawned on her that it could have resulted in me losing my life, we went to our knees in thanks at being granted another go.

Our motorbike transported ourselves with a chunky toddler squeezed in between, a gigantic bag of dirty laundry wedged into the front basket, a backpack, and even a keyboard when we led songs at the English Centre. Journeys were never dull. When it rained, cement roads and dirt tracks often resembled gushing streams and people tried to shore up the pot holes and steady the surface by putting down sharp, tyre-piercing bricks, tiles, and cement chippings. Livestock large and small, together with small children, ambled into the road at any moment. Once we were going on our motorbike to a friend's house for supper in heavy traffic when two small children suddenly appeared in the middle of the road right in front of our motorbike. Slamming on the brakes, I managed to swerve in the nick of time but the skidding almost caused Mei to fly right off the back.

On one particular journey back home on the motorbike, the laundry bag worked its way loose and choice items of clothing proceeded to tumble out all over the busy main road. The locals were rolling around clutching their sides while I ducked in and out of traffic to gradually retrieve the offending items.

A motorbike was not the safest mode of transport for small children. Well for anyone for that matter. After helmeting up, our three-year-old was wedged in between my knees with feet resting on a metallic frame that covered the hot, rumbling body of the bike. Although she loved rides out and about with her daddy, there were the inevitable tantrums when amidst kicking and screaming and a severely swaying vehicle, we somehow steered home to safety.

Then there came one of the defining moments of our time in Laos. Upon returning home from a village church forty kilometres away, I turned off the engine and lifted my daughter off. Only to watch in horror as in a moment of dizziness after sitting for so long, she stumbled onto the piping-hot metallic exhaust pipe. Instinctively reaching out with her arm to cushion her fall, she was burned along and under her armpit. Children tend to go straight to sleep amidst trauma and this is exactly what she did while we applied all of the Savlon cream we had brought for burns from the UK. Although the wounds healed well, we started to wonder whether we should think about purchasing a car sometime in the future.

When it came to traffic and particularly motorbikes, we did get to see the most amazing things in Laos. There were the teens who congregated in front of our house after school and raced each other to the end of the main road while doing wheelies. There was also the habit of Lao ladies of wearing pink teddy-bear pyjamas while jetting around on motorbikes from morning to at least lunch time.

The remarkable feat of holding up an umbrella against the rain or sun while riding a motorbike was also a skill all local people have perfected. It really did take a lot of grace and skill not to let your brolly crumple up and blow unflatteringly across your face within two seconds. I know. I tried it.

Another high art form in Laos involved checking your phone while speeding along on your motorbike. I mean really checking, nose-in-screen surfing. You would be glad to know I never tried this. Life was too valuable. I even had to reduce my gardening efforts in front of my house as it was too distracting to some motorcyclists who would literally drive looking backwards for twenty metres or so. It really was a small wonder that even more accidents did not occur.

For many years, motorbikes required mirrors by law although we saw that they were also appreciated for checking spots or pulling hairs. Vientiane and other cities have started cracking down on helmet-less drivers and driving up one-way streets but when you consider the continued struggle with errant driving in other countries, it will take a massive coordinated effort to even begin to contemplate how to challenge mindsets and attitudes to driving in Laos.

One of the challenges was the common perception that movement was good and stopping for any reason whatsoever was bad. From the north to the south, we saw it was perfectly acceptable to charge straight out into the main road from a side road without slowing down, let alone stopping. This was because the local perspective was that whatever road you happened to be travelling on *was* the main road for you. Again, no arguing with that logic! After all, large, paved, intersecting roads were relatively recent things. It was perfectly acceptable to ply your way against the flow of traffic if that meant saving a few seconds.

One of the best things about Laos were the free right turns at traffic lights. This fantastic idea should be used everywhere in the world because with a little caution and common sense, they enabled traffic to flow. With free right turns, routes could be planned right across town without having to stop at all. One handy trick that all local people had down to an artform was skipping traffic lights by using the free right turn twice. After making your free right turn, you then did a U-turn to use the second free right turn to proceed straight along your original route.

One evening after work, a colleague and myself were riding our motorbikes home when I lost sight of him in the traffic. Spying a pesky red light coming up, I made a free right turn and slowed down to make my U-turn into the traffic going the other way. Suddenly, I found myself catapulted from my bike onto the cement of the road amidst a tremendous crunching sound.

A motorbike must have been tailgating me, failed to see my indicators, and careered into the back of me. There were shattered bits of plastic and glass everywhere from my bike. I had nasty gashes on my ankles and shins. All I remember caring about, however, was where my glasses were. I must have suffered concussion as I recall combing the cement for them only to find them still on my head. The other rider and his bike were totally unscathed. He was nevertheless incensed and immediately demanded money.

My colleague had heard the crash and rushed to see what had happened. My first thoughts were to get out of there as fast as possible before things escalated. A few people were gathering but luckily it was late and hardly anyone was around. Miraculously, my bike somehow still worked and I was very grateful that my friend happened to be there to accompany me home. No more skipping traffic lights!

Another time when I was on my way to pick up the children from school, I spied a minivan hurtling down a steep side road towards my car! The only thing I could do was veer into the middle of the road while avoiding oncoming traffic. The next thing I heard was crunching gravel and squealing brakes as the minivan lurched to a stop just in time before the junction. A cloud of dust covered my car as I whizzed by. I pulled over to let my heart return to normal and breathe a prayer of thanks. The minivan sped past as I resumed my journey.

A few seconds later, vehicles rapidly started slowing down. As I approached, I could see that a terrible accident had just occurred. Three vehicles had crunched back-to-back into each other. Bonnets were crumpled, engines steaming, windscreens shattered. One of them was the minivan with the driver slumped unconscious over the steering wheel.

If driving in Laos left your heart in your mouth only several times a day, you were doing quite well. Even if you were the only driver on the road, constant alertness was in order. While driving on a familiar road in torrential rain in the mountains, I started to turn right and swerved in the nick of time to the cries of my family as I saw the swirling waters of the swollen river engulfing the track. We certainly had the angels working overtime.

Without a vehicle for our first few years in Laos, it was great to be loaned a bright blue 1964 VW Beetle for a meet-up with friends a hundred kilometres away from Pakse in Salavan. There was no aircon and push-out windows at the front only. Rather ominously, the owner insisted on a test drive beforehand to explain some idiosyncrasies. Once this was completed with flying colours, the journey was embarked upon, with a visit first to a Lao family forty kilometres out.

On returning to the car to continue our journey, it absolutely refused to start again. It would not respond to it being rolled down the hill for a push-start and we tried the ignition so many times the battery was about to give out. There was nothing else but for Mei to chat a while more with our friends while I sat nearby, prayed, and pondered what to do. There was no emergency car assistance in the south of Laos and the only option was to beg friends to tow us back. After an hour or so, I decided to have one final go at starting the engine and it roared first time into life. Perhaps even cars needed a rest sometimes, even if only after forty kilometres.

As we traversed numerous hills and valleys, single lane cement bridges crossed gushing streams. Talk about timing but it seemed a huge articulated truck would always come trundling down the hill from the other side of the valley to meet us head on at each and every bridge. Our Beetle was no match for those monsters and so the opportunity to play chicken was declined, which meant having to slam the brakes on before each bridge to pull over and grudgingly allow the thundering vehicles by, caking us with red dust in the process.

On our return at a refuelling stop, the Beetle refused to cooperate again. After calling around, eventually someone arranged for a vehicle to come out and tow us back. With the wait being hours, we decided to roll down the hill into Pakse in neutral. We were only forty kilometres out after all. A bright blue VW Beetle was already quite a sight in rural Laos but what a hoot as grandmas on bicycles overtook us and peered in. Motorbikes zoomed by with someone we knew kindly offering to accompany us. He gave up after a few kilometres we were going so slowly. Eventually we slid onto level ground where the engine started again as if nothing had happened and we ambled off home to the odd sight of modern-day shepherds on motorbikes herding cattle home. That car was henceforth dubbed 'Lazarus' although we mysteriously declined to ever borrow it again.

We had long harboured a wish to catch a glimpse of the endangered Irrawaddy dolphins which lived in the part of the Mekong near Cambodia. Along with my mum who was visiting, we took a rumbling old bus from Pakse, and chartered a boat across to one of the islands in the Mekong. Once we found accommodation, a boatman readily agreed to take us to look for the dolphins. Our eyes took in his longboat complete with outboard motor. The rumours that crossing into Cambodian waters held a higher chance of spotting dolphins became true. Before our joyful eyes, a couple of the creatures came noseying right up to our boat before darting off.

Little had we realised that ominous black clouds had been forming overhead. Sure enough, heavy drops of rain began to pelt down. The boatman promptly hauled out a large tarpaulin sheet for us to cower under before revving up the motor to make a beeline for shore. Fear descended as we promptly found ourselves in a tremendous tropical storm in the middle of the Mekong River. Thunder rumbled and the rain fell so heavily as to prevent sight further than a few metres. Panic started to set in as the boatman started to bail out water. Help us, Lord! What was I thinking to bring a pensioner and toddler into such a situation? This was the same mighty river that in places was fourteen kilometres wide, as it journeyed more than 4350 kilometres from the Tibetan Plateau to the South China Sea.[13] There was a reason that the Mekong was known as the 'Mother River' in the Lao language.

After what seemed like an age, the shoreline came into view. Clambering from the boat onto the rocks, we ran for shelter underneath a massive concrete overhanging. Hearts thumping, dripping wet, and shaking with relief, we gave thanks to the One who had ultimately brought us to safety. The boatman had wisely made for the only shelter for miles, a crumbling docking station built by the French years ago.

---

13. The Mekong is the twelfth largest river in the world but by discharge, the tenth largest (Milton Osborne, *The Mekong: Turbulent Past, Uncertain Future,* New York: Grove Press, 2000, p17).

As the storm subsided, the night was rapidly approaching and we were miles from our guesthouse. In the drizzle, we found a makeshift restaurant where we ordered some simple food and shared our predicament. The staff called someone on their phone and three burly men promptly turned up with motorbikes to take us back. My mum had no idea of how to even get on a motorbike but this was our only choice! Meanwhile, it had turned pitch dark and we became separated as the three motorbikes sped along tiny elevated dirt tracks criss-crossing dark, sodden paddy fields.

The mighty Mekong River

As we lost sight of one another, imagine how worried the ladies were at being alone with a strange man in the dark in the middle of nowhere. Each of us said a prayer and we eventually arrived safe and sound at our guesthouse. The generator and the fans went out promptly at midnight but we slept soundly, exhausted but grateful to Him for His care and protection.

Navigating from A to B was always an adventure in Laos but learning to rest upon the provision, kindness, and help of others enabled a certain trust in the Lord, together with all sorts of unlikely connections. Conversations could be had while a motorbike was fixed, or yet another tyre was changed, or on a long bus trip. Inconvenient at times for sure but what was the rush? A kind word out of the blue, a prayer of compassion, a glimpse of Christ-like concern would have been less likely if we had insisted on our own vehicle throughout. Even when we did have our own car, we prayed that it would be a blessing. In hindsight, we are full of wonder and gratitude at the God who kept us safe in the journey and enabled us to meet so many different people from all walks of life.

Chapter 4 – The Search for Home

Fine bits of shattered glass rained down upon us from above. The landlord of a house we wanted to rent had just turned on the electricity mains and every single light bulb had exploded. We were warming to the idea of actually living there when suddenly, Mei realised there was no kitchen. 'Just cook outside,' was the landlord's quite reasonable response.

We loved how nearly everyone in Laos cooked barbecue-style over a brazier of hot coals outside their houses. It must have been hard work for the fire to be lit, food to be prepared from scratch, and then cooked, but it was so relational. Tantalising aromas drew in different members of the family and neighbours in stages over a few hours of conversation and relaxation as the world passed by. Although we loved a good barbecue every now and then, the thought of having one every day was not that appealing. The housing search continued.

The idea of 'home' in a country not our own was hard for us to define. We desired a place of peace, of refuge for our family, but also a place of welcome where people from all walks of life would feel comfortable. Our motivation was to live simply and integrate into Lao society without too many distractions to ourselves and the people who we came into contact with. With the gift of hindsight, we recognised how Father God guided us to the right place for a particular season of our lives. There was the place in the heart of community when we needed to immerse ourselves in Lao culture and get to know people; the quieter, more secluded place when we were tired and hurting; yet another place with Christian neighbours when we desired to connect more with the local church.[14]

---

14. While we desired for 'home' to be a place of comfort and safety, we had connections with both the poor and the privileged. In response, we tried to live simply, holding 'home' and possessions lightly, and reminding ourselves that part of our witness was looking to God for our satisfaction and well-being.

The most memorable thing about our first house was its ancient twin-tub washing machine. The landlord and previous tenant had neglected to mention that it was not earthed. When Mei reached in to pull out the lovely, fresh-smelling clothing, she found herself propelled backwards as electricity shot through her arm. Our characters clearly needed to be honed as we repeatedly forgot to pull out the plug, each time receiving an excruciating jolt. The one consolation was that in the tremendous heat, clothes dried in no time but not before ravenous ants had fashioned sizeable holes all over our finest items of clothing.

We tried not to allow such challenges to get us down too much but set about opening up the house as a place of welcome. In no time, English students were sitting in our living room and even the Singaporean Ambassador and his family popped around. It was wonderful to have a young lady who was training to be a 'house-helper' from a nearby vocational centre to practise at our place.

After finding out her birthday and that her home was far away in the north, Mei prepared a surprise cake at which she promptly burst into tears. No-one had ever done this for her before. The simplest things often had the most impact: taking the time to acknowledge another person, offering a listening ear, stopping to sit with someone, pausing to ask for and receive prayer. What great opportunities to get to know Lao people, their family, and friends. There were few better ways, moreover, of getting immersed in the Lao language.

A short time after we had moved to Pakse in the south, our house-helper graduated from her studies and was offered a job there too. We knew how hard it was to find employment in Laos outside of the family network. Someone needed to vouch for you, help you get inside the system, stand up for you, look after you. The job offer was good but a terrifying prospect for a single, teenaged girl who had rarely been out of her village. Hardly anyone from her ethnic group lived in the south.

She showed great courage to accept the job offer but later told us that knowing we were there helped her make that decision.

We also needed accommodation in Pakse and found a house for rent that was not yet fully built! We were assured that with a year's rent paid in advance, the building work would be completed before we arrived. The piles of red earth outside would be transformed into a lush green oasis of a lawn. Curtain rods would be put up with shelves installed in the kitchen.

You may have guessed that on our arrival with a toddler and our life's possessions, there were no curtain rods, shelves, or a blade of grass. On closer inspection, taps did not work and the toilet overflowed. Whenever we washed, the water turned brown from the fine red dirt that got into everything. Rainwater collected on the flat roof of the bathroom, causing black, fuzzy mould to sprout inside.

It was a challenging start. The customary one year's rent had been handed over and the landlord's help was no longer quite so enthusiastically offered. Meanwhile, while talking to a church leader, a wall fan worked itself loose and spun right off, leaving one dumbfounded but calm gentleman sitting centimetres from where the whirring blades came to a stop. Gradually, we plucked up courage to venture out and ask for help in our faltering Lao. Mercifully, some basic things got fixed. Local people were glad to offer advice and assistance. By clambering up onto the flat roof, the putrid water and rotting leaves could be swept away, which reduced the dampness and mould inside.

Mei boldly visited the local shophouses and market to see what could be done about curtains. A Chinese-speaking merchant was promptly discovered and some lovely yellow floral curtains were selected at an agreeable price. After a few days, the curtains were delivered. They were different lengths. When this was pointed out, the seller declared that if Mei wanted things just so, she had better get her curtains made in

Singapore. We still have and cherish our wonderful Pakse curtains to this day.

A large group of labourers congregated outside our gate signalled that the time had come for the neighbour to access our garden to carry out a 'simple renovation' of his wall. What was not mentioned, however, was that this involved digging a crater for a septic tank and toilet extension in our garden. Imagine boisterous builders working four metres away dawn-to-dusk, seven days a week for a couple of months. Poor Mei and Keziah as I could at least escape to work. The neighbour quite understandably made a habit of coming in and observing the workers, and from all the shouting and regular shaking of fists, they got on like a house on fire.

Once this work was finished, an army of workers eventually arrived to lay down a lovely lawn of grass and some resemblance of peace was restored. The water no longer turned a deep brown every time we washed. The landlord redeemed himself by supplying ten banana trees and even someone to dig holes for them. Within no time, the banana trees grew, providing wonderful shade and regular offerings of fruit. The downside of the trees, as we would soon discover, was that nothing on earth could remove the stain of banana sap.

Speaking of bananas, it was very tough to pass the friendly *roti*[15] seller on the road outside our house without buying a few of his wonderful snacks. We soon got talking and discovered his part-Indian, part-Lao heritage. Gradually, he shared more of his challenging life. His wife had run off leaving him with two sons, one of whom was disabled. The *roti* seller literally glowed when at Christmas, we presented him with a gift of a special sign and menu for his stall. Soon enough, his children and

---

15. Lao people find the 'r' challenging in this Indian-origin word. *Roti* is a delicious fried crepe-like snack with lashings of condensed milk on top. Extras can include Nutella, chopped banana, or pretty much anything else you fancy.

their friends mustered up the courage to come to our garden to play and learn some English.

With little greenery to enjoy in central Pakse, our garden was the talk of the tightly-packed Lao-Vietnamese community living in the surrounding ramshackle wood and cement houses. As soon as we opened our gate, all manner of folk would rush over, stroll in, and wander about, generally ignoring us and enjoying their personal park. The neighbouring aunties also found our outside wall by the kitchen a most delightful place to lean against and long bamboo benches were soon installed. Raucous laughter and animated conversation filled the long, balmy afternoons.

After a few months, however, the children mysteriously stopped coming. This was strange as everyone always had such a good time. Perhaps someone had warned them to keep away from the foreigners? When we passed by their homes to investigate, we eventually discovered that it was all because of our rapidly growing banana trees. To the children and a lot of Lao people, the large, swaying leaves resembled *phi* or spirits reaching out to grab them. No wonder the children stopped coming. When we trimmed back the foliage, the children soon returned.

Together with banana trees, our Pakse landlord had also planted a few papaya trees. As the fruit grew and ripened, our anticipation of partaking of this delicious food grew to fever pitch. Imagine our dismay when we returned home one day to find that the landlord's father-in-law had let himself in and chopped down the choice papaya. All was forgiven, however, when he returned later to kindly offer us half of it.

There were also huge coconut trees overhanging the house, providing soothing tropical beauty and much-appreciated shade. We loved how approaching storms would be signalled by a sudden temperature-drop and eerie stillness except for the rush of breeze through the branches.

One night, a tremendous crash caused us to bolt from our beds. On inspection, a hefty coconut had deposited itself in the garden where it had cannon-balled into the tin roof and rolled off, thankfully when no one was around. Although we never heard of anyone getting injured by falling fruit, our toddler was tasked with playing well away from the towering trees.

'Coconut tree' by Keziah Whetham

Every few months, we would watch in trepidation as small boys climbed high up into the coconut trees, armed with ropes and machetes, to dispatch the fruit into waiting nets and sale at the market. Not a few items of fruit would conspire to smash into the roof of our house but at least we had a little warning of the impending blasts.

There was another smaller coconut tree in our garden that covered up the brash, cement wall of the neighbouring house. By using a ladder, I was able to inch up with a machete and arm outstretched to sever clusters of ripe fruit. A screwdriver helped make a hole to extract the juice with a straw. Then to everyone's amusement, I threw the coconuts high in the air to fall and crack open on the cement floor. The coconut 'flesh' inside was worth the effort and all for free.

One day, as I cut into a bunch of coconuts above me, a shower of fibre and dust dropped directly into my eyes. Temporarily blinded and in some pain, I stumbled inside to wash out the debris. I asked Mei if the neighbours had been burning rubbish again as the living room was filled with wispy smoke. Her concern was instant as there was no burning, no smoke, and I was suffering from blurry vision. I was scared to close my eyes in case I could no longer see when I opened them. I needed to see an ophthalmologist urgently but how in the south of Laos?

As we had no vehicle, a compassionate colleague at the English Centre insisted on renting a car to rush us to the Thai border an hour away. We only just made it across the Lao border before it closed at 8pm. We then had to hurry on foot across a considerable stretch of no-man's land to the Thai border. Imagine our dismay when we found the checkpoint on the Thai side had just closed! All the lights had been switched off and there was not a soul in sight.

Rushing back to the Lao side, we discovered that it had also closed meanwhile. The whole place resembled a ghost town. We were out in the open with a small child. There were no guesthouses for miles. With increasing panic, we called out and banged on the closed shutters of the buildings. After what seemed like an age, a disgruntled policeman in boxer shorts peered out. After begging him to stamp us back into Laos, he eventually agreed and with a sigh of relief, we were invited to part with a fine for the audacity of attempting a double border-crossing so close to closing time. Remarkably, our colleague and the man who drove us to the border had not gone too far back into town and with grateful hearts we returned home.

When I did eventually get to see an ophthalmologist, the blurry vision was put down to conjunctivitis which did not sound quite right. At just the right time, an ophthalmologist friend in Singapore agreed to have a look free of charge on our next visit. To our relief, no damage was found but a year's supply of recently-trialled medicine was prescribed to strengthen the eyes. The blurriness may have been an indicator of stress. No more climbing up coconut trees!

Living in the heart of the community brought a lot of joy but we had to put up with an incredible amount of noise and disruption. Soon after moving into our house, the neighbour set up a motorised wood saw ten metres away in front of his house and proceeded with admirable energy and ear-splitting efficiency to saw through countless logs all day long for months on end.

On another occasion, upon hearing wood splintering from the back of the house, I ran around to investigate and discovered our Lao-Vietnamese neighbours hacking down the mature tree that enveloped our house in precious shade. Horrified and with a loudly-beating heart, I relayed as calmly as I could that I did not want the tree to be cut. These protests were met with a shrug of the shoulders. The fact that the tree originated from outside of our wall made it fair game for the neighbours who deemed the spot perfect for the installation of an enormous satellite dish.

Speaking of noise, rain was a regular interruption. Whenever it poured on our tin roof in Pakse, all conversations needed to cease and amateur dramatics were the only way to communicate amidst the deafening roar. The interesting thing was that downpours usually occurred in the middle of the night. Sleep was impossible although the rain never lasted all that long. Water leaking in, however, was a common problem in all the houses we rented. We soon got used to positioning buckets at strategic points to catch the drips.

In lashing thunderstorms, however, buckets were little use against the wind-driven rain which would pour in through the window frames and walls. Woe betide you if any cherished books, toys, important papers, or extension cords had been left on the floor the previous evening.

Any sort of playground equipment in 2009 was next to impossible to find, especially outside of the capital. In Pakse, I would often take Keziah to a tiny German-funded park near the river. Although the equipment was rusty and the slide terminated about a metre off the ground, it was a soothing, quiet place and Keziah always begged for another go.

Imagine my excitement when one day, I spotted a homemade, wooden swing frame for sale on the roadside. I rushed over to bargain out a deal in my best Lao. The seller turned out to be a brother-in-law of our landlord. Our friend's father in Thailand thoughtfully fashioned a lovely swing seat out of wood to make the set complete and hours of fun for a little girl.

When it eventually came to the time for us to leave Pakse and vacate our house, I offered the swing set to a friend with small children. He readily agreed and popped round to pick it up. Suddenly, my friend and I were accosted by the man who had originally sold it to me along with his wife. They were furious to put it mildly. The whites of their eyes flashed as they angrily gesticulated and remonstrated. My Lao could not keep up with the torrent of words hurled my way. However, my rather bemused friend calmly talked the situation through with them, asking questions and taking time to consider the angry responses. We eventually deciphered that I had not in fact bought the swing set but struck an amazing loan deal and now had the audacity of giving the equipment away instead of returning it.

When we moved back to the capital, Vientiane, we helped take over the rental contract of a family who were leaving the country. This was mutually helpful as foreigners needed to cough up a year's rent in advance, and refunds for 'unused' time were a rare thing indeed. The only problem was the house was in a dip which meant water cascading in every time it rained. Our daughter, Keziah, had a great time splashing around in her boots although the mosquitoes breeding off the stagnant water were always a worry.

Fun in the floods

In no time, conversation and laughter filled the house. Sitting together on the floor, we shared local and international food, while practising English and Lao with the students from our classes and colleagues from the English Centre. Days were filled with the children's friends from school along with their parents. At Christmas, we put on a festive party for the children and Mei read the Nativity story.

In time, we also got to know the people in the markets and roadside stalls nearby selling *khao biak* (thick noodles in broth – literally 'wet rice'), *khao soy* (vermicelli noodle soup with minced meat and bean paste), and *bing jin* (kebabs smothered in dry, spicy sauce – literally 'Chinese fried'). A smile, a greeting, a question, a kind word. It was about being aware of the potential for deeper things to emerge in the everyday mundane, even while ordering food and choosing vegetables: the worry about a sick relative; the gloom of a downturn in customers; an invitation to a wedding or birthday. Christ-like availability, presence, and words acted as signposts to Him.

The house had a particularly small kitchen. It was so cosy that the gas tank for the cooker was stored outside and connected through a hole drilled right through the kitchen wall. One Sunday after returning from church, Mei tried repeatedly to turn on the cooker. On investigation, it became clear that while we were out, someone had hopped over the garden wall, removed the weighty metal tank from the pipe, and hoisted it over the wall. Purchasing a gas tank outright rather than changing it for a refill was quite an expense and must have proved too much of a temptation. We wanted our home to be open and welcoming but we nevertheless resigned ourselves to putting barbed wire on the outside wall.

We had always admired the house next door and we ended up renting it. There was more space for hosting film nights and events for our students. Hospitality could be offered to visitors and local people needing a roof over their heads and a hot meal. We saw more people dropping by to get something off their minds, seek counsel, or pray over something.

Moving house did not mean the adventures ceased. One morning as we opened the front door to a new day, our eyes took in a large tree that had fallen against the house during the night. We must have slept soundly! The landlord quickly mustered up a bunch of teenagers with machetes who proceeded to spend the whole morning chopping and clearing away the mayhem. How grateful we were to Father God for His protection and care. The landlord also owned a small shop and we intentionally shopped there to strike up good relationships and conversations with the whole family.

We often bowed our heads while walking around the outside of this particular house. Not in prayer but to avoid catching our heads on the razor-sharp edges of the air-conditioning units along the house wall. It was not long, however, before I absentmindedly walked into one, narrowly avoiding stitches and having to teach with a laceration across my forehead, much to the morbid fascination of my students. It was a painful way to understand why our local friends put polystyrene chunks on the edges of their air conditioning units.

On a rather memorable Christmas Day, I was in the garden when I suddenly heard shattering and yelling. Running inside, I saw to my horror that the bulky wooden and glass cabinet on the kitchen wall had worked itself loose with my wife underneath trying to hold it up. Meanwhile, entire piles of stacked plates, cups, and glasses were hurtling to their destruction. Slowly, we managed to bring down the cabinet to rest on the kitchen worktop amidst utter carnage. It was not worth imagining what would have happened if one of the children had been underneath. With loudly beating, grateful hearts we went to join our friends to celebrate Christmas Day.

The recent arrival of our second daughter, Kaelyn, ushered in new adventures. Without going into too much detail, cleaning a young child when nature calls could get very messy and we often employed the direct method of a bar of soap and running water from the sink. When we heard a heart-stopping crash one evening from the bathroom, we found Kaelyn sitting in the middle of the shattered sink which was now in small pieces on the floor. Water cascaded out from the broken pipes on the wall. She had tried to be helpful by employing most admirable climbing skills and crawling into the bowl to clean herself. We were not a little amazed and grateful to Him that she was not harmed in the slightest.

Shattered sink

We always joked that when my mum came to visit, we would have an adventure. Once, we borrowed a car because we wanted to take Mum to climb up to the top of *Patuxai*, the 'Victory Arch', in the heart of Vientiane. The climb was good exercise, the history of the arch was interesting, and the views were magnificent. When we returned to the car, however, I discovered that I had somehow conspired to lose the keys. We retraced our steps, panicked, prayed. Nothing. We resigned ourselves to abandoning the car and taking public transport home. Just then, I spied a group of soldiers nearby. Summoning up courage, I asked in my best Lao if they had seen any keys. Looking me up and down with a stern gaze, one of the soldiers held up a set of keys. I was ecstatic and probably embarrassed everyone by pressing some notes into the man's hand.

The striking 'Victory Arch' in Vientiane

Another time when Mum was due to visit, we were having dinner with a group of people for a friend who was leaving Laos. We would then head off to the airport to pick up Mum in an ancient truck we had managed to borrow from the English Centre. Before heading to the airport, Mei presented our friend with a farewell gift in a locally-produced, hand-made paper bag. The truck, however, refused to start. Time was ticking and our hosts urged us to take their car instead. Abandoning the truck, we sped off to the airport with some trepidation. Would the exposed battery on the truck be stolen meanwhile? It had happened before.

All went well with Mum arriving on time with all her bags. On reaching our house, however, Mei started to panic when she could not find the house keys. True to form, I had not brought mine either. What had happened to them? The keys must have slipped into the bag containing our friend's gift!

We called and called but our friend did not pick up which was strange and uncharacteristic. What was going on? It was pitch dark and getting on for ten o'clock. We could not get into our house and there was nothing left but to go back to where we had dinner and beg a place to sleep for the night. If our friend was shocked at seeing us at that hour, it was with utter calm and graciousness that she ushered us to the guestroom to rest our weary heads.

The next day we were grateful to see the truck still in one piece. It started immediately. We called up a local handyman friend to help us try and break into our own house. The spare set of keys was the goal waiting inside. Scaling the garden wall with barbed wire on top was the first step. Once accomplished, our friend spied an old-style aircon unit jutting out from the back of the house. After dismantling it right off the wall, he vanished headfirst into the impossibly small cavity to save the day. We discovered later that our friend to whom we had given the gift had her bag snatched the night before, with gift, our keys, and her phone inside.

All in all, Laos was a remarkably safe place to be. We were more scared of fire than thieves. Someone in the night kept setting the dry grass alight in front of our house and by the electricity pylons. Then they just walked away. Was it a carelessly discarded cigarette, someone burning rubbish, or something more sinister and deliberate to scare us to move out? It was horrifying to wake up to see the charred ground right across the land in front of us.

When a neighbour's house caught fire, huge clouds of black smoke billowed out. Frenzied people threw furniture and valuables out from the upstairs balcony. The city's one fire engine was in attendance and we kept a close eye on the wind. A change could have brought stray sparks on to our side of the wall.

Since the night I spotted smoke wisping from an extension plug in Keziah's room, my nightly routine involved checking the electrical items around the house and especially in the girl's rooms. The houses we rented had a lot of combustible chipboard along with old and haphazard wiring. Although lightning conductors were in evidence, appliances were seldom earthed. Even with surge protection, we still conspired to lose a fridge to fluctuating electricity.

Looking back at all the houses we rented over the years, it was utterly amazing that not one had a spirit shrine. We were very thankful for that. It would be an unusual house indeed not to have a shrine. Not only houses but hotels, shops, schools, and factories were sure to have a shrine somewhere on the property.

Spirit shrines were everywhere and resembled wooden or cement doll or bird houses raised on a post outside the building. Although one writer claims that they were usually empty as they represented 'unembodied forces',[16] it was not unusual to see tiny Buddhist and Hindu-like figurines placed inside. On the platform outside the spirit house, offerings would

---

16. John Holt, *Spirits of the Place: Buddhism and Lao Religious Culture* (University of Hawaii Press, 2009), p.18.

be placed which included joss sticks, a glass (always filled with red Fanta for some reason), sticky rice, and bananas. An umbrella was often positioned to shield the structure from the sun and rain.

We saw shrines that seemed more like ramshackle huts or shelters on the forest's edge to elaborate, glittering houses resembling a Buddhist *wat* or temple. This indicated how Buddhism was and continues to be understood and lived out in Laos through devotion to the spirits. For example, the guardian spirit of Vientiane is said to reside at the Buddhist temple of *Wat Si Muang* close to where we lived in Vientiane. Each day, we would see droves of tourists waiting in line to pay their respects to the spirit before seeing the city.

We often came across vertical bunches of twisted, colourful, shiny paper in caves or at the base of sacred pipal trees which were signs of spirit worship. Aware of the role and meaning of snakes in the Bible, we could not fail to be a little intimidated by the *naga* or water-snake spirits which were represented everywhere, entwined around the lampposts and especially on buildings and bridges near the Mekong.

It was clear that the spirits had a hold on the Lao people who were devoted to appeasing them, sometimes with consultation from a *mor phi* (spirit doctor). Many Christians we met had a keen sense of the spirits. One couple solemnly informed us that they had decided not to rent a certain house as they had seen a ghostly, headless man walking around inside. Another young man who stayed at our house calmly told me the next morning about the spirit of an old man who had entered his room while he was sleeping. No one stayed in our house after that story got out. It did not help that all people in Laos seemed to love watching ghost and horror films.

We would often arrive at our workplace all ready to teach English to the sound of eerie, repetitive, off-key music with percussion which indicated a kind of Lao-style séance was taking place at the house opposite. It was an unsettling thing to have as classroom background noise. Although we knew the spirits were under the lordship of Christ, they were not to be underestimated. Mei, particularly, was uncomfortable with the shrines, as her family background before Christ had been in Buddhism with an idol in the house. We acknowledged how important the spirits were to the Lao and did not belittle their beliefs and stories. However, we prayed that all of us would not become weighed down by fear but speak and live out words of life and encouragement that pointed to Christ.

Although never our experience, it was not uncommon for landlords to insist on being allowed entry into the compound of rental houses each day to present offerings at the spirit shrine. They would thoughtfully explain that it was as much for the good fortune of the people renting as themselves. Our good-natured friends in Pakse resigned themselves to leaving the front gate unlocked during the day for the landlord to come and go but someone must have been watching. While the couple went to the back of the house, their motorbike mysteriously vanished from where they had parked it inside the gate.

The Christians we met over the years had different approaches to the spirit shrines in their homes. Some were indifferent, some ignored them as inevitable, some felt uncomfortable but put up with them, some were determined to have them removed. One person hauled the hefty cement shrine from the front of the house and laid it down on the ground among the shrubbery at the back. This was a bold, almost symbolic act which might have attracted animosity or even recrimination from the landlord and others. No one seemed to bother. Other friends tried a softer approach, planting all manner of creepers and plants to grow over and cover the shrine. Try as they might, however, all the plants kept dying. Sheer coincidence or spiritual significance?

In many ways, our search for home was a search for peace, a place to retreat to, recuperate, and reach out from. There was much contentment in knowing that our various homes were a refuge and a welcome place for many local and expat folk over the years. Even if a fan, sink, or cupboard fell down every now and then.

Chapter 5 – Studying the Art of Connecting

We yearned to get to know Lao people and made a point of visiting anyone we could, starting with the homes of the local staff at the different English Centres where we worked. Being a teacher seemed to satisfy everyone who asked who we were and what we were doing. Being the first to walk across the room, be friendly, and initiate conversation was so necessary in Laos where it was entirely possible to spend entire days without having to see, let alone spend time with, anyone else.

We also tried to regularly attend the local churches to get to know people, understand and respect local ways of doing things, improve our Lao, learn local songs and worship alongside local people. Many churches had plastic chairs or pews for everyone, although some provided mats for sitting on the floor. In such churches, a few chairs were reserved for leaders, the elderly, and guests.

Humble village church

Although we were always treated with the utmost politeness, we preferred to sit on the floor with the masses instead of on the chairs that were invariably offered.[17] We found it was much easier to get to know people who were in closer proximity.

Whenever we planned to make a car journey far away, we would try to think of a local person who would not be able to afford the bus and offer them a lift home. This took us to far-flung villages dotted around the capital, the mountains of the north, and the plains of the south. We soon got used to local-style directions with very approximate distances and landmarks. These visits were a great chance to connect with families who appreciated the care and attention their son or daughter was receiving from us.

Typical Lao village scene

---

17. 'High' and 'low' are extremely important visual markers of respect. Status is shown in how 'high' you sit, whether on the floor, a plastic chair, a large wooden chair, or on a stage. Those honoured with a chair usually sit at the front or side with a few others or even alone. Choosing to sit on the floor could have caused embarrassment as the church could be seen to not be looking after us properly.

Where there was a church in the villages, we asked permission of the village head to organise arts and crafts, songs, and games for the children in the building. Having the humility to respect authority in this way usually resulted in a measure of goodwill extended to us. There was often a tangible sense of how the people we visited valued our choosing to be with them. In thankfulness, everyone would share wonderful refreshments and watch the graceful, traditional Lao dancing put on for us.

With an estimated population of just 7.4 million[18] in an area the size of the UK, Laos felt refreshingly uncrowded with the fewest number of people in South East Asia (2.5 per cent of the total population). You felt the space as soon as you left the plane. You got the sense of open spaces with people widely dispersed. Only around 10 per cent of the population lived in urban areas such as Vientiane and Pakse. An astonishing 85 per cent of the population were involved with some sort of agriculture.

Many people we met over the years juggled studies or work in the cities while popping home to the countryside whenever they could to help out with the family farm. However, the terrain often made travel challenging with the flood-prone plains giving way to fierce mountain ranges, forested ravines, fast-flowing rivers, and spectacular karst formations. All this made meeting people very challenging not to mention the communication issues with forty-seven ethnic groups listed in the government's census.[19]

We often marvelled at the generous, no-walls inclusivity of the local people. No groups, no divisions, come-one come-all, the more the merrier. We longed to have more of an approach to life like this.

---

18. I used 2021 stats from https://www.unfpa.org/data/world-population/LA (accessed 21 February 22).

19. Holt, *Spirits of the Place: Buddhism and Lao Religious Culture*, pp.7,8. This figure varies wildly according to source. Although the Lao language is the unifying national language, many people do not speak, write, or read it at all well.

Once, we were invited to a waterfall by a local friend who was one of the leaders at an organisation that worked with disadvantaged children, a work close to our hearts. It would be *muan* (fun) with other local and foreign people we knew. When we double-checked with the foreigner in charge of the organisation, he was horrified. It was a team-building day that he had put a lot of work into planning for. It was not just for anyone.

Another time around Lao New Year, a close local friend invited us to a project where he worked in the countryside. It was a good chance to relax and get to know some other Lao families. As we pulled up in our car, the foreigners running the project were standing at the entrance. I remember thinking how unusual it was for them to be at work during the holidays. Their mouths literally fell open as they recognised us. As more people arrived, it quickly became clear that like barbarians, we had barged in uninvited to their official New Year's staff party. They were not best pleased. When another local friend invited us to a 'coffee hour' at a foreigner's house, we finally learned our lesson and politely declined!

Although we sensed that Lao people preferred togetherness, that did not necessarily mean that verbal communication was expected to happen. The sight of people staring silently and transfixed into their phones was tragic. Yet what was different was how the people we observed preferred to do this while sitting close together in a circle. Together alone. Was the internet responsible for decimating verbal communication, with couples, friends, and families choosing their gadgets over each other? I was not convinced. The choice of opting out and tuning out instead of being willing to engage with others had simply been made infinitely more distracting and accessible. All courtesy of boredom, the internet, and the addictive action of swiping a screen.

On the other hand, we were delighted at how the Lao script had finally made its way into apps and websites with unprecedented access to people, information, and faith resources in local languages. Rather than printing out songs for times of fellowship, friends shared lyrics on social media and sang them from their phones. An unintended boost for the environment too.

The lack of a shared language was another challenge to meaningful connection. Although English was a basic skill within the Lao education system, there were few opportunities for people to hear themselves string together sounds, words, and sentences. It was always amusing to observe foreigners with some Lao conversing with Lao people who had some English, resulting in a quirky stop-start, sing-song linguistic concoction. We often found ourselves doing the same.

What an amazing opportunity for English speakers to connect with local people in gentle friendship, compassion, and support. What a window of opportunity for English speakers to get trained in teaching English and meet this resounding need through their vocation.

It is very difficult to just go up to people and strike up a meaningful connection without being treated with the utmost caution and even rejection. Teaching the English language gave us a context and valid reason for 'being' in certain spaces with particular people at specific times. Teaching enabled meaningful connections with hundreds of students, along with their families and friends. Teaching allowed us to stand alongside government, academic, community, and business figures. More on the treasure of teaching in a later chapter.

All this meant that having even the most rudimentary Lao language unlocked a world of perspectives, thought patterns, and a tremendous amount of goodwill. We saw how the Thai language was similar to Lao and widely understood so why bother? However, we could sense just how appreciated Thai speakers were when they adapted a little and chose to use Lao instead. One way of loving 'the stranger' was learning and using the heart language of local people.[20]

---

20. Framing the process of language-learning as hospitality is the intriguing angle on witness covered in David Smith and Barbara Carvill, *The Gift of the Stranger: Faith, Hospitality, and Foreign Language Learning* (Michigan: Eerdmans, 2000), p.10.

It did help that, on the whole, local folk were extremely gracious and looked past language mistakes to the communication that was happening and the relationships that were being expressed. Early on in the language-learning process, I remember my mouth literally falling open in amazement as my Lao tutor handed me list of expressions with the word *jai* or heart. A culture with such beautiful and expressive heart language was clearly a deeply sensitive one. Consider some of these *jai* expressions:

- *khao jai* – to understand as something enters the heart.
- *dee jai* – to be happy because you feel good in your heart. Switch the word to *jai dee* and it means 'generous' because you have a good heart.
- *sia jai* – to feel disappointed or sorry for someone is like your heart is lost.
- *tok jai* – to be shocked or get a fright is like your heart has dropped.
- *jai yen* – to be calm and composed is to have a cool heart.
- *jai hon* – to be impatient or angry is to have a hot heart.

The humbling thing was that although we quickly started conversing in Lao, it was only after around *five years* that we started to feel we had a handle on the language, let alone lead songs and staff meetings, or counsel people. To this day, we still have difficulties praying in Lao as honorific and ritualistic words and phrases need to be used.

We often found ourselves scratching our heads over the Lao words we encountered while reading an article or a story. After slowly sounding out the words 'com-pi-u-DER' and 'Fes' from the Lao script, everyone would fall around laughing as it suddenly dawned on us that we were using English ('computer' and 'Facebook'), albeit in uniquely local ways. Loving our neighbour as ourselves involved much laughter at ourselves and how ridiculous life seemed at times. In humility, we needed to remind ourselves that we were guests and learners in a country not our own.

Although English speakers are well-used to English being spoken in all sorts of ways, I often wonder how our Lao language actually sounded to Lao ears in real time. I could only imagine from the reactions of local people that it would include a mixture of amusement, surprise, and genuine pleasure that anyone would bother.

Learning the local language plunged us into culture, history, and politics which ushered in new ways of understanding the people and country. When the communist government took over in 1975, the Lao language underwent a kind of levelling to reflect a utopian classless society and vocabulary was barred that signalled status.

One of the startling ways of talking about 'I' we encountered, for instance, was *kha noi* (literally 'Little Slave'). Add *doi* the very polite 'yes' before this term and it meant something between, 'Certainly, Sir' and 'Yes, your Highness'. Although understandably banned from 1975, these terms were always under the surface and often heard when people were in need before God or someone of higher status. One writer on Laos shockingly asserts that the one place where *doi kha noi* continues to be actively encouraged is in the prisons.[21]

Again, in an effort to eradicate class, the jarring *jao* for 'you' is used when addressing an elderly person, someone in government, a friend, colleague, or a child. The people we interacted with tended to avoid such directness unless they were asserting themselves over someone else. Unless you were unable to keep a lid on your anger, other times for *jao*-like directness were if you were in a safe and familiar situation such as among family and friends at home or talking to a child.

Attempting to dismantle the class structure also meant that familial terms such as 'uncle', 'younger brother', and 'older sister', were encouraged

21. See Christopher Kremmer, *Stalking the Elephant Kings: In Search of Laos* (Australia: Allen & Unwin, 1997), p.76. We saw *doi kha noi* used much more in the south of Laos, where the people we met seemed to be much more deferential.

from 1975, often supplanting the need to use *jao*. Even *khoi* for 'I' is often replaced by a familial term or nickname. Talking about yourself in the third person took some getting used to but was great fun: 'Daniel will meet younger brother at the English Centre.' This roundabout approach was much more preferable to the uncouth, '*I'll* meet *you* at the English Centre.' All of this meant that anyone learning Lao was in the unenviable position of needing to be a prudent judge of age, context, and ironically status from the onset.

Although very beautiful and meaningful, first and family names (e,g, Siriphone Thammavong) could be long and were only used in formal situations such as schooling, certificates, or documents. Our friends and colleagues were secretly delighted when we sought out their 'real' names and called out to them from across the office. Short and funny nicknames were used for almost every other situation. These include the ever-popular *Noy* (Small) and *Joy* (Thin), used by both men and women. *Tui* (Fatty) and *Pa* (Fish) were also very common. English nicknames were also becoming more popular with some evoking car or motorbike brands such as 'Vigo', 'Fino', and 'Focus'.

Our students had a lovely way of positioning a 'Mister' or 'Miss' (in Lao or English) before their nicknames resulting in delightful combinations such as 'Mister *Xang*' (Mr Elephant) and my personal favourite, 'Mister Boy', which always brings a smile to my face. I was often called 'Mister Daniel' although Mei points out that 'Miss' was not as common for her, probably as the final 's' sound does not occur naturally in the Lao language.

We liked the way many people called us 'Older brother Daniel' and 'Older sister Mei'. Less so how many folks insisted on calling us *ajaan* (teacher). Although technically describing a professor rather than a 'normal' teacher, we understood the term was intentionally over-respectful, a one-term-fits-all used in hierarchical contexts. We soon found ourselves using *ajaan* to address anyone remotely older and wiser than us, especially in Christian contexts.

Deferential terms of address needed to be employed with anyone older, unfamiliar, and in a (potential) position of power or authority, even if the person had barely graduated out of secondary school. Take for instance the young immigration official at the border who had barely started shaving. Being intentionally overly respectful may just smooth a potentially protracted process and enable me to get home quicker. The constant analysis and outworking of 'respect' and its impact on language and behaviour made getting to know people that little bit more fascinating and challenging. We sure made many gaffes along the way, being overly direct in situations where we needed to be deferential and overly respectful when we could relax.

Any navigation of respect in Laos needed to start with the *nop*, a greeting that avoids taboo touch and maintains distance. It involved putting both hands together as if praying, with your fingertips more or less in line with your nose. It was an ingenious way of not only greeting someone but showing respect, excusing yourself, apologising, and saying goodbye. Perhaps globalisation was responsible for the curious habit of urbanised men to first offer a *nop* then swoop in for a hearty handshake. With other men only of course. Greeting everyone twice in this manner really boosted the atmosphere and camaraderie.

We were relieved to discover that there really was no need to *nop* everyone at all times, especially children, family, and friends. It was quite an artform, however, to work out precisely who to *nop* to and when. The formality of the situation along with status and age had quite a lot to do with it. Be ready to *nop* during local festivals and times of celebration and sorrow.

One rule of thumb was to ensure to return a *nop* when another adult offered it. An 'If in doubt *nop*' approach communicated a willingness to be humble and amenable. This often meant having to stop whatever it was that you were doing, and put down bags, cutlery, or a motorbike helmet. Naturally, there were times when this was impossible and a sincerely-offered one-handed *nop* was better than none at all.

It was quite an unusual thing to witness people speaking out and asserting themselves in public. The Lao way we saw was quieter, gentler, indirect, and graceful. It was always preferable to have someone else speak or vouch for you. This was part of being respectful in a relational hierarchy but we really did sense a lovely, genuine shyness and reserve with local people.

In formal situations such as the office, we got the impression that opinions and perspectives were seldom asked for or given. Silence was assumed to be respect, understanding, agreement, and loyalty. Nevertheless, people relished opportunities to discuss things, often as a one-to-one or in smaller groups, and preferably in their heart language.

At the same time, people would go out of their way to help, invite, and include others. Early on in office life at the English Centre, I remember discussing with my local colleague a financial request someone had made. I was about to dismiss it when he pointed out that the person had used *kor* (a polite, strong, pleading 'please') to frame their request and so his needs should at least be considered.

We loved the way in which local folk were experts at holding everything in balance, accommodating and accepting while not necessarily being impacted, committed, or influenced at all, especially by anything inconvenient, unenjoyable, unfamiliar, or foreign. In a hierarchical, relational, and community-orientated society, why risk isolation and rejection by asserting your individuality?

This caution was understandable when you looked at the heartbreak of Lao history and how the country was often in the hands of dominant nations with people suffering in situations out of their control. A lot of the alienation of ethnic groups was stoked by the French approach to colonialism which imported a Vietnamese hierarchy into administrative positions.

However, it was the devastating, years-long military campaigns by America (and North Vietnam) which utterly destabilised and crushed both the elite and people in the countryside.[22] Soon after our arrival in Laos, we visited the UXO[23] museum on Kouvieng Road in Vientiane. Few know that unparalleled in the history of warfare, more US bombs were dropped on Laos during the Vietnam War than on Germany and Japan combined in World War Two. Let that sink in.

A lot of people on the ground would have had no idea why they were targeted. US policy dictated that warplanes could not return to base with their payload. Indiscriminate carpet bombing meant that munitions were dropped randomly on people who had nothing to do with the fighting. Imagine children playing in the dust, farmers tending their animals and crops, families washing in the river, elderly folk resting from a day's work and watching the world go by.

The thing that really disturbs me was the design of the munitions: just one bomb casing contained hundreds of tennis ball-sized *bombies* (coined from English). Picture millions of *bombies* fully intended to be strewn randomly in all directions over a big area. Yes, troops would be 'disrupted', but everyone and everything else was obliterated too: someone's child, sister, mother, or grandfather. Those that survived the bombardment fled into caves and the deep jungle.

The evil was only multiplied by the catastrophe of a third of bombs

22. It is hard to imagine the horror of the violence on all of society. See Holt, *Spirits of the Place: Buddhism and Lao Religious Culture*, p.5.
23. UXO = unexploded ordinance. This must-see 'living' visitor centre is run by the Mines Advisory Group (MAG) with a prosthetic limbs department. A sobering, humbling experience.

not detonating upon impact. Meanwhile, a predominantly agricultural society continues to grapple with UXO embedded in the earth, forests, and river beds. Think about the hand-reaching inquisitiveness of the child. The scraping and burrowing of the scrap metal collector. The downward strike of the famer's hoe. The excavation of the rumbling digger for the new road. The furrowing nose of the hungry cow.

The tragedy of stumps and mutilations were countless. We saw commendable work happening with organisations such as MAG and Halo Trust striving to clear the land of UXO. Even with President Obama pledging millions of American dollars for clearance, this was a drop in the bucket. There remains an ongoing, urgent need for worldwide focus and funds to secure justice for the Lao people and their land. The thing is that with a will, the evil of UXO could be solved once and for all, by the powerful, the rich, the movers and shakers.

One man we knew hurled himself into the heart of every football match although he lacked an arm and had mangled lips from picking up a bomb when he was younger. He was a gritty, tenacious character and I guess he had to be. Imagine our happiness years later when we discovered he had married a girl from the very first local church we used to go to in Pakse. When we visited the couple in their traditional house, their faces brightened immediately as they showed us the rattan brooms they made to supplement their farming. It was a poignant moment when they pressed a child-sized broom into our hands as a keepsake.

Even with Mei being Asian, the way we dressed and walked made us stand out. Wherever we went, children and even adults would shout out, 'Falang, falang' (literally a French person, now used generally for any foreigner). Although annoying and not very polite compared to the more refined *khon dang pathet* (person from overseas), we seldom sensed any animosity towards us as foreigners. Maybe the people we encountered were far too polite to express what they may have sometimes felt in their hearts.

Occasionally, we heard stories from friends about officials who had visited their villages warning against foreigners and the way they used money, 'assistance', and material goods to win trust and ultimately leverage control and change for the worse. When we visited a far-flung village in an area with hardly any Christians, we were shown a well that had been dug by a Christian organisation. It had a lovely blessing inscribed into the concrete. Yet, foreigners, 'development', and Christians were treated with much caution when they posed a threat to the familiar, peaceful, and unifying aspects of the Lao culture and way of life, Buddhism, adherence to the spirits, and the nation itself. What this meant at a village level is that Christians could well find themselves ostracised, denied documents, and generally being treated quite shoddily. One friend calmly showed me the room where he was detained for two nights during Christmas. The punishment was for gathering for a church service without permission. 'They hit me,' he told me with a bitter smile. We came across similar stories time and time again.

A caution and suspicion towards foreigners is underlined in the words of the Lao national anthem that declares the right of the Lao people to be their own masters, and never allow imperialists and traitors to harm them. Lao independence and freedom were to be diligently and fiercely guarded.

One of our daughter's friends was from a powerful political family and surprisingly invited her to her birthday party. When we eventually got past the gatekeeper and strolled through the lovely, manicured garden, the menfolk smiled and courteously invited me to join them for a customary drink by the pool. Politely turning down this opportunity, my daughter and I went to find her classmate. Catered food was laid out beautifully on tables outside. The weather was perfect. Not too hot and humid with clear skies. Children from school were happily milling about.

As we passed the classmate's mother, she loudly asked her daughter in Lao why she had invited a foreigner. She may not have realised that we understood every word. Perhaps her volume and tone were completely intentional, a kind of communal apology for a taboo breached. Her gut-reaction underlined the simmering ill-feelings of a political and historical reality. Even at a child's birthday party.

Quite understandably, we saw how there was deep safety, peace, and comfort for many local people in familiarity and predictability. Anticipating and avoiding situations that were unfamiliar, awkward, or out of one's control not only 'saved face' but could literally be self-preserving. Even in the life of faith, we found it striking how the content, order of service, and many of the songs in the Lao Evangelical Church had remained much the same from its inception.

Whenever we had groups of students around, we would find it so endearing how everyone would wait for a secret signal before excusing themselves at the same time to leave together. People tended to use a specific approach, particular words, and body language when it came to public life. Status-quo, 'group-think', and silent loyalty to whoever was in authority were key.

That was why communist-inspired meetings encouraged throughout society could be so unsettling because for local people relationship-preservation took absolute priority. In such meetings, everyone was encouraged to say something, usually negative, about someone or something else without incrimination. At least not in the meeting itself. The issue was that in such societies, voicing one's opinions seldom happened in isolation or without some sort of effect. Better to work alongside one or two trusted local colleagues to meet and talk with individuals and small groups.

Although often very tricky to navigate, times of hardship and suffering presented opportunities to connect with people through sensitive, practical compassion together with simple presence and if appropriate, words of comfort, love, and hope. It was about being sure to rejoice with people in times of happiness and weep beside them in times of sorrow.

I vividly recall bustling out of an English class in 2013 when my students clamoured around and breathlessly related how a Lao Airlines flight had crashed into the Mekong with everyone lost on board. As the news sent shockwaves around the country, we discovered our friends' son and daughter-in-law had perished. In unthinkable suffering, his parents somehow managed to share with everyone they met, including prominent Lao business leaders and officials, about their faith and that of their son and daughter-in-law. Our Buddhist house-helper also wanted to talk and Mei had opportunities to share about the hope we have of life to the full now and after death.

Some of the most amazing opportunities to share hope were with the sick. Although foreign healthcare professionals were rarely granted permission to work in local hospitals, foreigners were surprisingly allowed to visit sick people there. It sure made you vulnerable and odd looks were thrown our way as we walked along the corridors. Yet the remarkable thing was that although we stuck out like sore thumbs, no one ever challenged us as to why we were there. Or insisted on accompanying us. Perhaps people had enough of their own worries to deal with.

The reality is that hospital visits could put yourself and others in danger but opened all sorts of doors. Tact and wisdom were vital as words and actions could easily be misinterpreted and spoken accusation held weight. People were even imprisoned after being charged with acting as false doctors when they prayed for someone who died afterwards.

At the English Centre, times of singing worship songs, sharing stories, and praying for one another led people to be encouraged, witness, and step out in love. We would sometimes invite local visitors to sit in and it was amazing how particularly the songs impacted people and prompted them to ask more about what we were singing about and who we were singing to.

There was the time a colleague shared about a friend from her village in the north who had come in from the mountains to the city hospital to give birth. When we heard she was having difficulties and needed a caesarean, we took a team of people in to pray, with practical gifts and toys for her other children. She gave birth to twins shortly afterwards and returned home. Much too quickly it seemed. Over lunch a couple of weeks later, we choked on our food when we heard she had died with an infection.

The heart-rending faces of children with swellings on their head and neck were etched on my memory. Little to no research had been done into possible causes. Were there dangerous insecticides and chemical infiltration of the food chain that caused these dreadful swellings?

We heard from colleagues about a child and her mother who had been brought in from the mountains bordering China to a hospital in Vientiane. We gulped when we saw the dreadful, evil swelling on her little neck. She clutched the soft toys we offered and all we could do was pray. It is peculiar how no-words were better in such situations. As a whole bunch of people searched for someone with the expertise to intervene, no one could be found and nothing could be done. All the mother wanted to do was return home and wait. Everyone was in tears.

Becoming ill in Laos could be very dangerous as adequate healthcare provision was both scarce and expensive. A colleague from the English Centre told us sorrowfully about her aunt who had been feeling unwell and needed to make the long trip to the city hospital. As it was extremely hot and humid, we took in a standing fan, some other small gifts, and prayed for her. A few days later, we heard she had been sent home as there was nothing more that could be done for her. She died shortly afterwards. This story was repeated time and time again.

Road accidents were all too common. There was the teen who had been discovered 'lying down for a long time' in his village. He had suffered multiple leg fractures after trying to escape from the police and tumbling from his motorbike. After being brought the thirteen hours by bus to the city hospital with his mother, pins were inserted into both legs with the miraculous provision and expertise of a foreign orthopaedic surgeon. The operation was a success but the young man had months of physiotherapy to undergo.

A team of local and expat people continued to help, visit, and pray. In local hospitals, patients were responsible for their own food and bedding, meaning relatives literally set up camp beside the bed with pots and pans, fans, and roll-out mats. Being in the big city far from their village, mother and son were disorientated amidst the hustle and bustle of the hospital, medical information, and lists of expenses. What an opportunity to show kindness and compassion.

As their needs were provided for and people prayed and shared about Him, the patient and his mother both professed a stuttering faith. Love, healing, and hope had become a reality for them but there was still a long way to go. They must have missed home terribly, however, as they suddenly walked out of the hospital without telling anyone and returned to their village long before the physiotherapy was due to finish. In such stop-start, heart-rending situations, we often found ourselves praying that the good work He had initiated would be brought to completion.

After one of our colleagues shared how his six-year-old nephew had been hit by a vehicle and paralysed from the waist down, we immediately rushed to visit him at the hospital. He had been brought many hours into Vientiane from the provinces. We managed to pray discreetly and have a risky but positive faith conversation with the father who was a soldier. For months afterwards, a whole team of people prayed and we were amazed when the boy made a full recovery and the faith of everyone involved increased.

While making my way out of the hospital after visiting our colleague's nephew, I heard the terrible noise of a girl screaming out repeatedly, *'Jep hua, jep hua'* (my head hurts!), in agony along the crowded corridor. As I passed by, I heard my name. A man who I assumed was her father was calling out to me but I did not recognise him. This happened all the time as people knew me through the English Centre. In the commotion, he explained how his ten-year-old daughter had suffered a brain haemorrhage. Her life was clearly in danger and the available healthcare was likely to be inadequate. The family were desperate for help and a miracle from Him. Feeling utterly helpless, I promised to pray and hurried out to find out if others knew about this urgent need and were willing to help. Still unsure how the man knew me, I asked Mei to investigate and it turned out we had once played football together. On opposing sides.

Joining a team of friends and the leadership of an expat doctor who was also a friend of the girl's family, we set about praying and researching what could be done. Finances needed to be raised urgently for what was bound to be expensive surgery and long-term healthcare. I remember feeling impatient to meet the target personally and through our array of contacts but the doctor wanted this to be the opportunity for the Lao community to band together and act rather than rely completely on foreigners. He had more faith, nerves of steel, and patience in what was a very precarious situation.

Thankfully, local people did get involved and after a year of disappointments and cancelled appointments, ground-breaking 'gamma-ray' surgery was finally organised in Thailand. After a nerve-racking operation, the girl recounted how someone who called Himself

Jesus had been standing alongside her as she lay alone in the hospital. She made a full recovery and we thank God for this miracle and how our two families were bonded together in friendship.

As we think back over the years at how we approached connecting with local people, we committed countless blunders and experienced a lot of joy and sorrow along the way, often at the same time. It was about learning how to stumble gracefully. Yet doing so in His strength. We persevered in using English teaching as a means to being signposts for Him in and out of the classroom and we saw all kinds of fruit. We continued walking across the room and reaching out in partnership with people and organisations. We kept learning Lao, encouraging others, sharing stories, songs, and food, talking to Buddhist people, visiting the sick, moving in practical compassion, and praying for people. We kept brainstorming ways of creating opportunities for ourselves and our colleagues to be signposts to Jesus in natural, everyday, relevant, and sensitive ways.

Eyes would often light up when we talked about deeper things. Prayer was often asked for and appreciated. When rain was prayed for during a terribly dry period, how it poured immediately afterwards in a truly miraculous answer which people still talk about today. People would often seek us out to delve more into faith matters. In other situations, an immediate, stony silence would fall if we mentioned *anything* to do with faith.

We took encouragement from one veteran in Laos who described the work as still clearing away the rocks from the ground. The task of upcoming workers in Laos is to persevere in partnering with Him in wonder, humility, patience, creativity, and courage as stones continue to be removed and fresh opportunities open up and present themselves.

Chapter 6 – The Lao Smile

It did not take long for us to make many connections among the people we met every day in Laos: the eager students, jovial market-sellers, serious officials, the boisterous classmates of our children, inquisitive neighbours, our various landlords together with their extended families.

We loved how the people we interacted with seemed to exude a readiness to smile, be welcoming, friendly, and willing to take time for others. Often, we were shocked to see teeth full of cavities behind the smiles, or none at all. An old lady who used to ask if she could gather plants from our garden always had a smile for us, revealing the red-stained lips and teeth of an avid betel nut chewer.[24] More recently and perhaps an indicator of development, awareness, and disposable income, we noticed that smiles increasingly displayed braces, often multicoloured.

It certainly seemed to be a cultural rule of thumb that people needed to be very calm, smiling, and cheerful at all times, at least in public. The Buddhist quenching of 'self' and 'desire' as causes of suffering, certainly had an influence on being in control of one's emotions. How odd foreigners were with their many words, animated facial expressions, and energetic body language.

Inevitably, there were people who were really unhelpful or rude, indifferent to us and the people around them, or simply demonstrated a terrible attitude to life in general. Thankfully, these experiences were few and far between and we relished the easy light-heartedness of the local people.

After noticing my usually cheerful local colleague smiling but looking drained, I discreetly asked him if he was tired. The immediate shadow

24. The chewing of a package of powdered lime, betel leaf, tobacco, and flavourings such as cardamon and cinnamon.

that dulled his eyes and vehement denial of all tiredness showed that unintentional offence was caused. He had taken my care and willingness to help to be a criticism of weakness.

Public outbursts of rudeness, emotion, and anger did of course happen from time to time. When they did, it was truly shocking because they were so rare and the place to show your true colours was behind closed doors at home. We saw how this control of the emotions led to a lot of gossip, complaining, frustration, anger, and even violence behind the scenes. People did need an outlet when they had been bottling up their emotions and smiling for hours, days, weeks, or longer. An all-too-common scenario we continually experienced was people trying to enlist us to 'pass on' anonymous messages of discontent to others.

Perhaps letting off steam also contributed to the wicked sense of humour we saw in a lot of local people, which was often very unnecessary, harsh, and unkind, particularly from those who called themselves Christians. Often, a gentle rebuke would be needed when issues of marriage, purity, faithfulness, and sexuality were undermined and made fun of.

One house we rented stood three metres away from a woman who almost lost her voice whenever she screamed incessantly at her husband. Which was often. Would she have acted differently had she known we could hear and understand every word? Perhaps not. In a society which keenly felt shame rather than the guilt of wrongdoing, the 'sin', error, or mistake may bring about emotions more to do with embarrassment, dishonour, and indignity. These reactions, however, would often only be felt when the behaviour or situation was called out publicly, even though the whole world knew all the details already.

As you may imagine, trying to stay calm and cheerful all day in the intense heat was not always particularly easy. However, we soon discovered an infinitely helpful expression. This was *bor ben nyang* ('It's nothing', 'No problem', 'Never mind'). Try it. It rolls off the tongue and sums up the easy-going attitude to life that all people in Laos aspire to, at least outwardly. My students explained to me that the impermanency of everything in the Buddhist mindset meant that you had to be carefree and hold things lightly. The *bor ben nyang* mentality that we encountered in Laos made other Buddhist nations look positively stressed.

In fact, people said, '*Bor ben nyang*' so often that when something *was* serious or *did* matter, it took some resolve to remain patient, understanding, gentle, and willing to keep working with people. Outer calm, inner irritation. There was no use in questioning, discussing, or arguing about *bor ben nyang*. Naïvely, we once asked what the opposite of *bor ben nyang* was. The answer, of course, was, 'There isn't.' Once, we accepted the *bor ben nyang* approach as the way things were, life became more bearable. In fact, the whole *bor ben nyang* mentality became so addictive that we soon found ourselves thinking, saying, and living it.

If at all possible, *bor ben nyang* needed to be accompanied by your best smile at all times. It was well worth practising this last point in the mirror. A smile in Laos could well be happiness or a greeting, but also rejection, annoyance, shyness, acceptance, embarrassment, or insistence. Even hatred. It would be an error to discard the Lao smile as superficial.[25] In a society that placed a high value on graceful, indirect, subtle, and non-verbal communication, the smile and the eyes were one of the main utensils in our toolbox of grace and love for local people. You could fake a smile for upholding the cultural principle of being cheerful but the eyes often unmistakably pointed to the soul. What an unforgettable experience to see the combination of a broad, genuine smile and shining, hope and love-filled eyes in the faces of those who had met Christ.

---

25. Thinking through how to offer Jesus as truly good news for people with a very different culture, language, and understanding of life forms much of the content of this evocatively titled book. See Jane Fucella, *Behind the Smiles: Tales from Life in Thailand* (Exeter: Onwards and Upwards, 2017).

Knowing the local language certainly assisted with interpretation of the smiles around us. I often helped out at local schools and one day I entered the staffroom as I needed to print off some worksheets. The local staff were on their break, smiling and laughing. What a carefree atmosphere. However, it soon became clear that the staff were discussing and sharing some very strong criticisms of another foreigner. No one realised I could understand every word. In such intense and awkward situations, the *bor ben nyang* approach was a great help, often more of a gritting of teeth in a resolve to stay positive and rise above the negativity.

Helping at local schools was a great way of making
meaningful connections in the community

Consider an everyday task such as using your laptop. This paragraph, for instance, was partly written with speech-to-text software which needed the internet of course. Only the electricity cut in the middle of the writing task. Clench your fists and grit your teeth in frustration? Not at all. *Bor ben nyang.* Smile and shrug your shoulders. All was well with the world.

Switching gears, I headed to the now-dark bathroom and flicked the light switch on and off. And remembered. Perspiration began to glisten on my forehead with the fans now also off. Gathering up the laundry, I attempted to turn on the washing machine. And remembered. With no electricity and internet, I gathered joy and resolve in rescheduling the day which involved an intense discussion with spouse and boss and not a few texts to notify colleagues and friends. Suddenly, the electricity came back on and I happily reapplied myself to the initial task at hand.

The open secret to coming out the other side in such situations with your sanity somewhat intact was the God-given joy of holding things very loosely and knowing that tasks one and two were impossible to carry out until the day after tomorrow. Tasks three and quite possibly four could be ticked off quite soon with a bit of luck. We marvelled at how finely tuned local people were into this perspective.

Consider the joys of the mailing system in your country. We saw signs of a basic residential address system being formed in Laos but mostly in the capital. Most houses did not have an address apart from a main road nearby and a landmark such as a factory or ancient tree. Most towns had a post office with post-boxes to rent yearly for next to nothing.

A nifty little trick was to get senders to put our telephone number on the outside of the letter or package and we would get a nice call in the middle of a staff meeting from a postal worker to come and pick up our letters. Saving this number was a prudent idea as no one introduced themselves in Laos and launched into whatever needed saying. It was also understood that anyone could hang up whenever they wanted, even in mid-sentence. Having someone call first saved having to randomly pop in three times a week to the post office to ask whether our parcel had arrived yet.

Picking up mail in Laos incurred a potentially lucrative handling fee which soared upwards if you received anything remotely heavy. It made for quite an expensive but reliable way of doing mail. Either you waited for a month or more for a letter from the UK, or you secured a post-box at a post office on the Thai side and waited two weeks but without the courtesy call when mail arrived, plus the hassle of a double border crossing.

Whenever it was time to send a letter, I set off bright and early for the post office, skilfully navigating a moon-like crater at the entrance. As I entered the building, I realised I was the only customer in the entire building. My eyes took in three members of staff huddling to the side of the front counter eating noodles or *pho* (obviously pronounced 'fur'). Perhaps they were interns from the local university? More importantly for my tick list, their welcoming smiles let me know that in no shape or form would they like to jump up and enthusiastically assist with my letter.

As I steered my eyes to the right, I noticed the nice lady that served me last time entering the room. I requested in my very best Lao that I would like to send a letter to the UK. Although there was a long, complicated word in the Lao language for the UK, everyone referred to the UK with a much easier, shorter word. This was the word '*Angkit*' or 'England'. Regrettably for the other nations of the UK, the same applied for the 'English' Ambassador and the 'English' Embassy.

The lady smiled, indicating she was ready to help. Acknowledging my request with a nod of the head, she asked in Lao whether I would like normal post or courier. Keeping in mind the high cost of sending anything by courier, I requested the reliable but slow Lao postal system. She then proceeded to leave the room. Just when I was wondering whether I had been abandoned, she swept back in, sat down and asked how she may be of assistance. I smiled and replied in my best Lao that I would like to send a letter to the UK by normal post.

I helpfully reminded her that 'the UK' or 'England' in Lao was the code 'GB' in her computer system. Explaining the various names of the United Kingdom to my students was always a headache. How did 'GB' correspond with 'UK' or 'England' for that matter? Indeed, I saw that she had begun looking for 'UK' on her computer. With my best smile, I sweetly reiterated that the code she needed was 'GB'. She then summoned her superior from 'The Back Room'. After an age involving three members of staff clicking and typing with eyes roving back and across the computer screen, I was dutifully informed that the code for 'UK' was in fact 'GB'. A nifty postal sticker was then expertly printed off, my letter whisked away, and I was motioned towards the payment counter clutching an invoice.

Wondering if the postal sticker was ever actually applied to my letter, I only now noticed the unusually high cost. Did the staff mark it to be sent by courier after all? As I handed over a wad of notes, I comforted myself with all the time saved in choosing not to return to the main counter to query the cost.

However, I did need to confirm that the letter was actually sent for posting. This I did in my politest Lao. The staff looked at one another dumbfounded. What did this foreigner want now? I smiled while repeating my query. Everyone relaxed and smiles were restored: 'Yes, of course,' was the immediate answer. I proceeded to thank the entire staff for their help. '*Bor ben nyang*. See you again,' I cheerfully called while backing out of the room, happy in the knowledge that I had posted my letter and full of resolve for the next challenge of the day.

For a while, friends at a local organisation helpfully allowed us to use their post office box in Thailand, assuring us that their staff routinely went to check and bring mail across and we would get a text if anything turned up. One day, we received a call from one of the office staff asking me to meet her. Not at the office but at the police station. It appeared that the police wanted to open some packages that were addressed to myself.

As Mei was at work, I loaded the children into the car and picked up the member of staff from her office as I did not know where the police station was. Her smile immediately let me know I was adding to her work responsibilities for the day. As I followed directions, I realised we were going to the immigration office on the Mekong River. It transpired that the member of staff who had gone to pick up the mail from the Thai side had wanted to save some money and went by boat instead. On return with his pockets bulging with small brown-paper packages, the border police had been understandably curious as to their contents.

I left the children in the car and on entering the police station, was greeted cordially with smiles all round. I was ushered into a small meeting room. So far so good. The suspect packages emblazoned with my name were brought in. I recognised my mother's handwriting. I was asked to open them and the doubtful contents spilled out. A handful of Oxford Reading Tree books and a *Guinness Book of Records* were uncovered.

Clearly not acquainted with the delights of Biff, Chip, Kipper, and the gang, the policemen examined every page of each book, reading extracts aloud from awe-inspiring numbers such as *House for Sale*. After an excruciating wait, the books were deemed worthy of entry in Laos and the mandatory photo-taking session ensued, first with myself with each book, then with all the books, and then with the immigration staff.

Agonisingly, it transpired that the big boss had left early and was not answering his phone. The policemen explained that they did not have the authority to release the books into my care. Just then, a master idea popped into my head: 'My children are waiting outside and they were so much looking forward to reading these books,' I truthfully explained in Lao. The policeman nodded understandingly and kindly allowed me to take three packages full of books but keeping one as a kind of deposit.

A member of staff from the office was entreated to return the next day to fill in forms and retrieve the remaining package. The thoroughness, politeness, and diligence of the immigration staff was exceptional. The Lao smile was employed throughout, no feathers were ruffled and, with a little patience, everyone got to benefit from the local-foreigner interaction.

Laos was one place it was easy to be a millionaire. The currency, *kip* (pronounced 'geep'), comprised of notes as coins were abandoned in the 80s. For many years, an ATM withdrawal of $100 would net you around 800,000 *kip*. This would usually be in 50,000 *kip* notes. Occasionally, however, it would be in 20,000 *kip* notes, and a backpack rather than a wallet was urgently called for.

Not too long ago, you would be sure to annoy people by purchasing something small with a 50,000 *kip* note. You would be left standing for ages while the salesperson asked around for smaller notes. In recent years, we saw how 50,000 *kip* notes were still valuable but had become the norm. Even the 100,000 *kip* notes introduced in 2011 did not raise too many eyebrows in the urban areas.

Unsurprisingly, despite the billboards everywhere encouraging people to use the national currency, large transactions such as rent or purchasing a vehicle were always carried out in dollars and sometimes Thai *baht*. For many years, until banks became more reliable and sophisticated, these transactions would often be up front in cash and in a large bag.

We loved using *kip* but it was impossible to change outside Laos for other currencies. This meant continually having to keep an eye out for good exchange rates, particularly for the Thai *baht*, as a lot of travel, shopping, and healthcare involved crossing the Mekong into Thailand.

Around the time we were moving from Vientiane to Savannakhet, new government banking and currency exchange regulations meant it was prudent to close our *kip* account. When I withdrew the money, my heart sank as the staff member gave it all to me in 50,000 *kip* notes rather than the usual 100,000 *kip* notes for large amounts. What on earth to do with so much paper money? I could not very well stuff it all into pillows or carry it around in sacks. I was on a motorbike too. As all Lao people do, I stuffed the notes into my backpack, wore it on my front, and wore a jacket over the straps.

There was hope for what to do with this huge amount of paper money as a month's deposit for our new rental house needed to be paid and the year's school fees for the girls were also due. There was an amazing discount if fees were paid upfront for an academic year, but would such a large quantity in *kip* be acceptable?

Marching into the school administration office, I still recall the ashen face of the school accountant as I literally emptied out a backpack of tightly bound piles of 50,000 *kip* notes, all of which needed to be carefully counted and verified. As the national currency it had to be accepted but the accountant's smile communicated in no uncertain terms that I was not the most popular person in Laos that day.

After I eventually escaped with my head still intact, the rental deposit still needed to be paid. We met the landlady of our rental house and with our best smiles, offered the deposit in *kip*. To our relief, her courteous smile communicated just a hint of annoyance, and she graciously helped us offload a few more million *kip*.

At one of the branches of the English Centre, there was a store room of sorts at the back containing a washing machine, shelves, and cupboards filled with all sorts of junk, maintenance equipment, and paint pots. Propped up behind the washing machine was a colossal, dust-covered, cobwebby, old wooden cross. It had been there for as long as anyone could remember.

After delving around to find out where the cross had come from, someone thought it could have been made by international prisoners as a means of supporting themselves. That such a potent symbol could have been allowed to be fashioned to that scale in communist Laos was astonishing. My mind's eye conjured up grim-faced expressions and perspiration as prisoners toiled with the wood in the searing humidity. I wondered if tiny glimmers of hope were felt as hearts contemplated the meaning of the item being assembled.

Surely this dusty legacy could be of use somewhere and yet all the churches we had contact with had crosses already. Searching further afield, a church leader in a neighbouring province assured me that they would appreciate the cross. At the next opportunity, I decided to embark on the risky endeavour of taking it there. The first surprising feat was actually being able to fit it quite comfortably into a minivan which was the only sizeable vehicle available to borrow at the time. The proximity of the cross to a large portion of the windscreen was rather disconcerting considering all the bumps certain to be enjoyed along the way.

The next challenge was what to do if stopped at one of the numerous police checkpoints along the way and the offending item was recognised for what it was. There was no question of hiding or covering it although it did look like a supporting structure for a roof. A likely tale. Added to this was the ever-present reality in Laos of the vehicle breaking down at any point along the road, usually in the middle of nowhere.

About a hundred kilometres into the journey, my heart sank as a policeman up ahead stepped out and waved me to the side as a checkpoint came into sight. Curt but polite, the officer confidently stepped forward smiling and oozing authority. Window dutifully lowered, driver's licence asked for, offered, checked, and returned. Destination queried and answered. The next question was unexpected to say the least: 'Are you travelling alone?' It was quite clear that no one else was in the vehicle. Perhaps it was an attempt at friendly chitchat. It was considered an odd thing in Laos to seek your own company. My friends were often incredulous that I would enjoy cycling on my own and often offered to accompany me so that I would not be lonely.

On this occasion, I confirmed with my best smile that I was indeed travelling alone. The advice was then offered that I should take my wife along next time. This unanticipated guidance was gratefully received as the signal that I was free to go. In no time at all, I made it safely to my meeting point and a rather controversial item was safely delivered.

As the church building straddled the main road, the leader shared how they were not allowed to display a cross on the outside of the building. Inside was quite a different matter. Although the building needed a cross, it was moving when the leader went on to share about another smaller, struggling church nearby but much further off the beaten track. They were facing testing times and could do with the encouragement of receiving the cross. A seemingly common, underutilised, and dusty item ended up being a treasure. It was with joy that I departed, a little less apprehensive about being stopped at a police checkpoint.

The Lao smile certainly helped smooth over some pretty awkward situations over the years although we often misread the smiles and cheerfulness before us. Even our local Christian friends got it wrong from time to time. We had set up a group for practising English conversation in which a local friend zealously pressed home her point about her Christian faith. Our lovely, gentle, Buddhist friend smiled throughout, graciously accepting the point. She never came back. Time and time again when we ventured into matters of faith, the light in the eyes of the people around us would vanish, replaced by a certain hardness.

The point is that it sometimes took real perseverance to walk with people. Months, even years would pass by before accurate 'readings' of cross-cultural communication and trust were built and people felt able to share deeper emotions and experiences, challenges, and struggles in ways they were comfortable with.

We continue to learn about all things Lao, holding things lightly, laughing at ourselves and situations, being humble, and realising that there is no destination to arrive at with communication. There are only people, created and loved by a God who longs to communicate with them. The amazing thing is that He often chooses to do so through us.

Chapter 7 – The Treasure of Teaching

Wherever we went in Laos, we were reminded that the English language was in demand. In far-flung villages, children would shout out, 'Hello!' and some random words they knew from school. In the cities, shy students would pluck up enough courage to venture up and practise a few lines of conversation.

Actually learning English, however, was not always taken all that seriously. Our friends explained that everything worth doing in life had to have an element of *muan* or enjoyment or it was not worth bothering with. Although I found teaching English enjoyable, it was admittedly not the most *muan* activity my learners could think of.

Over the years, however, we saw how teaching enabled access to all sorts of people: the urban, those from the villages, the wealthy and powerful, the poor and needy, the religious, the indifferent. All rolled into a hotchpotch of students ranging from privileged, spoiled teenagers with the latest fashions to those on scholarships; from monks with glistening, shaved heads and orange robes to government officials.

Monks collecting offerings of food from local people

These people would have seldom found themselves in a room together. Plenty of cultural norms, presuppositions, and prejudices jostled under the surface. Learners preferred to sit with their own gender. Younger learners showed respect and perhaps fear of older learners by giving them lots of space. Officials and professionals often treated other learners like little children. We had monks in our classes but it was strictly taboo to be in close proximity, let alone accidentally brush by or touch them. All chose to place themselves under our care for an hour or two, a week, a month, or a term. What a challenge, responsibility, and privilege. What a spur to reflect on what our faith was asking us as teachers to consider, live out, and communicate.

Although we yearned to share the hope that we had with our students, we took a respectful and cautious approach not only because of the so-called 'restrictive' context we were in but because of our beliefs in who we were as teachers and how we should go about our vocation. We took a middle road to witness, aware of the power of our influence in the classroom and cautious about seeking to include 'faith-related' content.

We had promised the Lao government that we would not 'proselytise', that is trying to coerce, persuade, and convert people in the classroom and at the English Centre. Visas, relationships, teamwork, goodwill, and whole projects rested on understanding, respecting, and keeping to such agreements. Long-term work by colleagues, partners, local people, and the local church would have been jeopardised through hasty and unwise attitudes, actions, and words. Unless learners, local and expat colleagues, and the community at large had agreed beforehand to faith-based content in our teaching, we shied away from using the classroom for this purpose.

We wanted, moreover, to link our teaching with the witness of integrity. We wanted to do what we said we would do; that is teach English. Whether students had paid a lot or a little (through a scholarship), all had signed up with the understanding that they would be learning English. Their investment of time and finance, trust, and hope in us to assist them would have been compromised if classroom time and the teacher-student power imbalance were used to dwell upon our faith and beliefs.

The teacher-student power imbalance was all the more pronounced because Lao society held teachers in high esteem. Teachers often acted as gatekeepers to educational support, opportunities, and pathways. Teachers had the authority to sway scholarship decisions, deploy focus and help in different ways, and determine important scores including whether learners passed or failed. We saw a pressure for students to be agreeable with the teacher in all things in order to maintain the status quo of peace, camaraderie, and progression in their studies. Perhaps extra teacher assistance and better grades for the 'best' students would also be thrown into the bargain.

We believed that making the English language needs of our students our top-most priority helped connect witness and integrity. We wanted to be professional Christian English teachers who were able and trusted to deliver quality teaching and learning. We also wanted the limited classroom time to be used effectively to cover materials, practise content, and ensure students understood. This meant that time needed to be put into planning our lessons. What were the aims of our classes and how would we achieve them?

That was why we insisted on people getting trained up in how to teach before coming to the English Centre. Having the humility, openness, and teachability to work alongside more experienced teachers was so important for both newly qualified teachers and teachers new to the country. We saw how empowering it was when leaders carved out opportunities for teachers to take a step back, reflect on, discuss, and develop aspects of their teaching.

It was important to let our students know more about the way we measured and assessed their English learning. We could not assume they were familiar with the different approaches we took to calculating their progress. Final scores could reflect attendance, punctuality, homework, writing, unit tests, together with mid- and end-of-term tests. Doing all of this in a consistent and fair way helped keep up standards but also our integrity of witness. Students were not seen to be more successful because of their powerful family backgrounds, teacher favouritism, or because of their keenness to delve in matters of faith.

Tests at the English Centre were also conducted a little differently perhaps to what many of our local friends were used to. Tests often seemed to be something optional in the local culture. Our hearts sank when learners suddenly said they would be 'busy' at the exact time of their test. We rapidly learned not to panic and rearrange everything but solemnly remind everyone that not completing tests meant almost certainly failing the entire course. It was remarkable how everyone would suddenly be available again.

We also heard that it was quite common in some local schools for certain teachers to walk out mid-test for fifteen minutes so that learners could confer or consult their notes. If your friend motioned to copy from you, it was your solemn duty to oblige. Now that is caring for others. Instead, our learners were seated individually in rows, far from one another and the reflective glass of the windows. Phones were put on silent, everything placed in bags, and left at the front of the room. The penalties for cheating (10 per cent deduction each time) were explained but there was always one who tried it on. One student elaborately feigned a terrible tummy ache and ran to the bathroom where he was caught with a friend from another class frenetically writing down answers on a scrap of paper.

After tests were thoroughly marked twice over and returned, we discussed with the learners how marks were lost or gained. We were keen that students could not only see and compare their tests but were allowed to keep them. If we whisked away the tests again after such a short time, it would have been hard for any student to reflect upon and discuss how they could improve.

Although the language needs of our students were our priority, we wanted our teaching to be signposts to Him. Surely our faith could impact the *way* in which we taught.[26] From the start, I noticed that learners said very little and simply listened to the teacher. What a dream set of students! Not so great for learning a language, however. I soon learned that the people in my classes were not only shy but cautious towards foreigners. Perhaps they were on guard because they had little idea of what to expect. Perhaps they had been solemnly warned against the negative influence that foreigners exert, particularly in regards to local religion and culture.

As foreigners, we were assumed to be Christian and there was no point pretending otherwise. Moreover, an internet search and some basic English would reveal the faith-based connections of the business where we worked. Doubly suspicious. It was understandable that we were looked upon with caution and scrutiny. A positive way of looking at this in terms of witness was that the way we carried out tasks and worked with one another would have been watched all the more carefully.[27]

All our learners were deeply immersed in Buddhist culture, which stressed that desire was the cause of suffering. Our wants should be quenched which called for restraint, self-control and calmness. No shouting out in class. In addition, the learners were used to teacher-

---

26. Apart from people noticing our Christ-like character, I was struck by how the way we set up and utilise classrooms, activities, conversations, and materials also reflects our faith and points to Jesus. See David Smith, *On Christian Teaching: Practicing Faith in the Classroom* (Michigan: Eerdmans, 2018).

27. I was so aware that particularly the busy, stressful, painful, intense times were incredible opportunities for witness to our identity in Christ. See Donald, B. Snow, *English Teaching as Christian Mission: An Applied Theology* (Scotdale, PA: Herald Press, 2001), p.73.

fronted lessons with little learner input. Their quietness, however, was a cultural way of affording respect to a teacher and an authority figure. Only more so as foreign English teachers in Laos were scarce and a valued commodity.

Faith-motivated teaching recognised that the cultural and educational backgrounds of the learners were beautiful and that the teaching approaches that I used and that were encouraged in the curriculum, may not work so well. What I saw as discussion, 'being yourself', speaking your mind, arguing your case, could be taken as showing 'desire', challenging the teacher, disrespecting your peers, or a lack of personal grace, tact, and intellect.

I had a tendency to get quite animated when I taught. Mime and gesture were necessary tools in the classroom but to my Buddhist learners who valued self-control, they may have been interpreted as overbearing and even aggressive. How embarrassing. To be respectful and accommodating to local ways of doing things, I tried very hard to be more aware of volume, body language, and facial expressions.

By learning Lao, I wanted to communicate the value of the local language but it was so helpful for understanding and assisting with the pronunciation hurdles my learners had with English. You already know about the lack of a final 's' in the Lao language, but that also includes the final 'z' sound (e.g. 'prize'). In addition, several consonants such as 'sh' (in shoe) and 'th' (in thin), for example, do not have obvious equivalents. Lao has a sound between 'v' and 'w' (e.g. try it with 'Vientiane'), but making a strong 'v' is often difficult (e.g. vase). Lao is also a tonal language and while English has no tones, it does have varying intonation. Infamous British dry humour, especially irony, often relies on intonation (e.g. 'That's great', could mean very different things depending on the 'music' of your voice).

From my classes, I soon noticed that learners rarely had the chance to disagree appropriately in English. The characters in the textbooks were flat and conversations were too short and often involved transactions such as asking or complaining at a shop, airport, or hotel. When discussion and disagreement inevitably occurred, my learners would often sound abrupt, impolite, or harsh without meaning to. Then everyone would be embarrassed. The room would be silent.

In response, I gradually tried to teach some appropriate vocabulary, intonation, and body language to enable learners to discuss and disagree respectfully with one another and myself through roleplay and teacher modelling.[28] It was my faith that motivated me to encourage students not just to learn how to disagree and complain, but to ask questions, show patience, work well with others, and learn to interact with other people who were made in God's image, not just a stock image in a book.

Being late seemed to be a national artform in Laos. Far from being endearing, it drove me to distraction. It was not too long, however, before we also learned to be late for all sorts of things. On closer inspection, though, it gradually became clear that a lot of people did manage to get to certain things on time and even earlier. No one was ever late for playing football. We heard friends relate with fear of local school teachers who locked the classroom doors at certain times. Local church was another place where we tiptoed in with fear and trembling whenever we were late, as the watchful eyes of the leaders surveyed the masses.

Hardly anyone turned up on time for my classes. I had explained the timings and the benefits of sticking to them. Other teachers docked percentage points for lateness. Was I not *muan* or strict enough? Was my teaching worth being late for? I wanted to improve the situation but continue showing patience and grace towards my students and the culture in which I was a guest.

---

28. It was good to be reminded to equip our learners with the type of faith-motivated language we wanted them to use. See Kitty Purgason, *Professional Guidelines for Christian English Teachers* (California: William Carey Library, 2016), pp.78-81.

Rather than wait for everyone to trickle in before starting, I instead tried to value and reward the two or three students who were punctual. I did this by using conversation warmers with tricky vocabulary that I knew would be useful and practical. In this way, I communicated the benefits of being punctual, not for the principle in itself, but in order for local people to make use of the very short, limited classroom time. Without having to create fear or lose my cool, those who were late knew that they had missed out.

I also started students on completing a 'Personal Learning Plan' which aimed to help them think through their strengths and weaknesses and approaches to learning English that may be helpful such as being punctual or jotting down new items of vocabulary in chunks of language rather than in isolation.

Acknowledging and welcoming the presence of every person in the room from day one was a great way of communicating God-given worth and dignity for everyone, for the duration of their time with me as their teacher. This included a high priority on memorising names and valuing the contribution of every voice, not just the teacher's or a few select individuals.

Mei and I tried to set up classes that were relational and respectful, where every student could contribute and have 'a slice of the teacher'. Over my time in Laos, I was painfully aware that teachers, including myself, tended to talk far too much. Encouraging 'student talking time' and turn-taking while minimising 'teacher talking time' were for the good of the learning process but also for the kind of kingdom relationships I was seeking to model and build. Ensuring that everyone participated and contributed was quite a challenge.

In response, I regularly carried out this simple but powerful activity to gauge who contributed in my classroom. I mapped the seating plan and names of learners. Every time I prompted someone to contribute, I made a mark by their name. Then, I started again but this time made a mark every time someone contributed without my prompting. The patterns and anomalies made for very interesting reflection and tweaks in my teaching approaches.

To encourage contributions from everyone, I found that student-teacher journals were a gentle, slower, and less intense approach for those who wanted to share more but not out loud or in front of others. I did not mark journals for grammar but tried to encourage fluency and openness through the use of questions. It was interesting how certain personalities would open up through the medium of writing: the visit to the hospital, the exams coming up at school, the argument with a sibling, or the uplifting song they just had listened to.

Although we did not proselytise using classroom time, it was clear that apart from the linguistic content, there were political, spiritual, and cultural messages in the curriculum we used. Secularism, materialism, consumerism, and individualism were often shown in a positive light that made me feel uncomfortable and want to open up to discussion with my learners. Where were there more positive aspects in the materials that could be highlighted? What about content related to hospitality, simplicity, generosity, forgiveness, and satisfaction?

The curriculum we used already avoided potentially controversial topics (publishers need to sell books!). Through the materials, however, it was not a stretch to encounter opportunities to discuss racism and prejudice, debt, broken relationships, and the human impact on the environment. Our learners would also often share things in class that they had picked up from social media. What about the tendency to say, 'Oh my God!', for instance? Surely such deeply sensitive and religious people would appreciate the opportunity to stop and ask whether that phrase was the most appropriate response available.

What an opportunity to model listening with openness and respect, while contributing a brief, quiet, faith-motivated, gentle comment to the discussion. Even so, we tried to stay well clear of politics, issues of justice, or religion, except in the most general of terms. We dreaded those times when an eerie silence would fall immediately when students sensed the invisible line had been crossed. As guests in a foreign country, it would not have been wise, respectful, or appropriate to dwell on such matters in the classroom.

It was amazing, nevertheless, how ordinary, mundane things in the curriculum could be approached or 'turned' to contemplate more meaningful things. A discussion, for instance, on the multicultural significance of 'bread' or 'light' had the potential to touch upon the spiritual.[29] In the same way, layers of meaning could be drawn out from dreams, allegories, proverbs, fairy tales, and poems.

Thinking carefully about 'intentional questions' linked in with the curriculum helped to gently prise open and coax learners to contribute and share more of the inner life with one another (e.g. 'What are you most scared of?', 'What is love?', 'What would you change about yourself?'). With a little assistance, even beginner students could tinker with simple language that pointed to spiritual issues (e.g. 'I am thankful for . . . because . . .').

The stories, conversations, and personalities presented in the curriculum were a start in presenting and practising target bits of language but were often limited and rather shallow. I felt that the lives and experiences of the learners before me needed to be acknowledged, valued, and utilised. In response, I often 'personalised' the materials in the curriculum by encouraging the learners to share from their experiences, and sharing mine too.

Although teachers, including ourselves, knew that learners needed opportunities to express themselves about things that were meaningful

---

29. 'Bread' could refer to an item of consumption or evoke ideas of world hunger, wastefulness, and the bread of life. 'Light' could mean a lightbulb, a candlelight vigil, or a symbol of good and evil. See Smith and Carvill, *The Gift of the Stranger: Faith, Hospitality, and Foreign Language Learning*, p.196-7.

to them, they were worried about the time-constraints involved in 'covering' the curriculum. These concerns did not always need to be in tension, however. Learning occurred as language was employed in natural ways. Take for instance a simple, rather superficial question in a textbook about how the weekend was spent. The time could be spent discussing rest and work, leisure activities, obligations, sacred days, prayer, meditation, and religious spaces such as a shrine, temple, or church.

Another example was a topic I taught from a popular textbook called *A Rule for Life*. The activity involved listening to four people talking about what was most important to them, completing notes, and answering some questions. Why stop there? I extended the activity by sharing my own rule for life which included putting God first in my life, along with playing football, and spending time with my family. Each student then wrote about their own rule for life. Some responses were cultural, some were spiritual, all were personal and authentic.

Personalising material in this manner not only helped the learners learn and practise language but provided a natural exchange of ideas, values, emotions, and convictions.[30] It was important, however, to strike a balance towards encouraging students to open up and talk about complex issues and the inner life. The serious needed to be blended with the light-hearted, together with language needs and everyday concerns.

Our students were from 'collectivist' or community-orientated upbringings. In contrast, a lot of the content of our learning materials tended to lift up the individual. In response, we learned to also extend heartfelt interest, concern, and prayer for the families, friends, colleagues, classmates, and neighbours of our learners ('How is your

---

30. It is striking that as integral, whole beings, our responses to life that characterise us as humans do not occur in isolation. See Smith and Carvill, *The Gift of the Stranger*, p.205.

family?', 'How was the harvest this time?', 'Did your family go to the temple at the weekend?').

We also used a lot of pair and group work in our teaching. Rather than relying on individuals to respond and complete tasks, we asked a mixture of individuals and pairs to read aloud, answer questions, and complete work on the board. We saw how important it was to give time for learners to work with each other and consult one another. Seating arrangements and groupings were tinkered with to provide opportunities for individual, teacher-student, and group work. Every time we asked a student to turn to a neighbour and practise a conversation, relationships were being prioritised and expressed. We loved using activities that could only be completed if students got up and out of their seats and talked to one another.

Whole-life witness to Him involved an above-and-beyond attitude, carrying out the work wholeheartedly, as working for the Lord, rather than simply for people.[31] We combined this with a welcome for people that communicated acceptance, patience, forgiveness, love, and compassion. A simple gesture which Mei and I loved to use was collecting and displaying a class list of birthdays, including ours, and without the year if people felt shy. We took a short time out in class to celebrate birthdays with one of Mei's sumptuous home-made cakes and a personal note of blessing. It was about being intentional about creating a community that spoke of and involved people in kingdom acceptance, love, and goodness.[32]

The relationships inside the classroom inevitably led into everyday life and we often bumped into and got to chat with students as we buzzed around town and many popped over to our house. We loved

---

31. It was good to earn the trust and respect of those in authority over us by being faithful even in the small things. How much more so for the Lord who we poured out our lives for (see Colossians 3:23-24).
32. It was good to be prompted to ponder what the kingdom looked like in my classroom. See Purgason, *Professional Guidelines for Christian English Teachers*, p.26.

offering hospitality to students and often spent time eating together. After the end of term, at Lao New Year, and Christmas, we organised get-togethers at our house and at restaurants which were so enjoyable. It was made all the more fun because we had no idea how to order the food and our students would take charge! We often had to anticipate wise replies to the inevitable questions such as why we chose the country of Laos. Loving the country, its people, and teaching made answering this question so much easier and truthful.

The gift of availability was offered to learners before and after class and often in our own free time. Rather than individual connections on social media, we liked forming class groups online for transparency and building relationships. Responding to requests for help and tricky language questions could then be accessible to all and favouritism was minimised.

Healthy boundaries, energy levels, and personal living space often helped to shape our availability. Being alone with a student behind a closed door was unwise even if others were milling about. Meeting students at a noodle stall or café was often the wiser option. Offering the gift of availability inevitably led to interruptions, delays, and detours. We tried to plan for margin in our daily activities to allow time and compassion for the unexpected situations that suddenly popped up.

Another way of making genuine points of connection with our students was by keeping an eye out for upcoming local Buddhist and international festivals and sacred days. Rather than presenting or dwelling upon a particular viewpoint, we would give it a brief mention and ask the students one or two open-ended questions (e.g. 'When do you give presents in your culture?', 'What did you do at the temple yesterday?').[33]

---

33. Is the way we talk about faith and religion integrated and natural or forced and stilted? See Purgason, *Professional Guidelines for Christian English Teachers*, p.6.

In this way, we learned about the significance of the revered temple nearby where Buddha was said to have leaned against a particular tree. We learned why people like to float candles down the Mekong and release fire lanterns into the sky.[34] We had a riotous time flipping pancakes and discussing Lent on Shrove Tuesday (Buddhism also has a Lent-like period). We read a moving account of St Valentine and shared what we were grateful for on Thanksgiving. These curious 'foreign' celebrations often popped up in the curriculum and the media the students devoured while we longed to understand more of the meanings behind the local customs.

In all of this, a rule of thumb was to make sure that conversations were two-way and that people felt heard. Having an open attitude to others meant being genuinely inquisitive about perspectives and opinions, local ways and customs. This often included being prepared to listen to different angles of the discussion, even when it was a little uncomfortable for me and perhaps other students too.

With extreme caution, we gently sounded out Lao people who were perhaps open to studying the Bible using English. We took a real risk by asking a successful businessperson who could have easily complained to the authorities and made our lives very difficult if she had taken offence. However, she loved our discussions, always bringing lots of great questions to the table. In the middle of reading Genesis of all books, she declared she was ready to receive God into her life! As a good work was started in her life, she became uncomfortable about some dubious business practices she was caught up in and began thinking through how things could change for the better.

Another Christian young man was always incredibly keen to study

---

34. This is a striking opportunity to release and send away any wrong committed over the previous year. Imagine the wonder of a dark sky and river lit by thousands upon thousands of lights. Some Christians have carefully utilised these incredibly important rituals to witness to Jesus who has forgiven sins once and for all.

the Bible in English and never missed his weekly session. In his words, it charged up his spiritual batteries. His English improved so dramatically that he went from a failing student to passing his end-of-term test. However, it was sobering when people 'missed' what God was offering them. After months of studying the stories of Jesus with one particular young man, we read the Parable of the Sower together (see Matthew 13). I was praying that he would see his need for God in his life but without hesitation, he declared that he was good soil. One thing about the Christian faith was that hope was never far away in these difficult times. We continued to pray and to persevere in love for the people around us.

We highly valued partnership and humility. We were never designed to plough alone. Our time with students was limited. We had restricted energy, specific skillsets, interests, and roles. Some planted, some watered, but it was key to be reminded that it was God who made things grow.[35]

We recognised that many of our actions and conversations better upheld teacher integrity if carried out by someone else unconnected to the classroom and the English Centre. Although we loved regular contact with the people we met, we tried to link them up to appropriate people in local faith communities.

Although many learners were able to hold deeper conversations in English, it was good for them to also talk with local people to gauge local ways of expressing and explaining deeper things. For those with lower levels of English, deeper conversations needed to be in their heart language rather than English. Although we spoke Lao, we grappled with biblical Lao and 'Christianese', especially when we did not use the language as a local person would.

---

35. God's people need to be vigilant towards minimising individualism, competitiveness, and pride. How freeing and humbling to be 'merely' one of His servants, with a particular task, and through whom people come to believe (see 1 Corinthians 3:3-11 and Romans 12:3-8).

Over the years, we were very encouraged by the fruit of teaching. There was the deep satisfaction of knowing countless students who grew in ability and confidence in English and used it as a stepping stone to study and work opportunities. This brought blessing into their lives, their families, and the development of the country. Money, stability, and options yes, but also confidence, dignity, and self-respect. Not to mention new ways of seeing themselves and the world. Still today when we chat with former students, many thank us wholeheartedly for helping them become who they are today.

In many ways, the restrictive context of Laos was one to be grateful for, that witness to Him was not simply jumping in and saying and doing anything we felt like. Being co-workers with Him for the kingdom meant patiently thinking through the ramifications of words and actions and considering how to be sensitive signposts without compromising integrity. We wanted to guard the dignity and worth of others rather than treat people like targets. We wanted to acknowledge and celebrate everything that was beautiful and good about Lao culture.

It was encouraging to remember that our belief system, Christian or otherwise, and the way we lived it out in everyday life, had the powerful potential to influence those who learned English with us along with the content of our lessons. We can all recall a teacher who we remember for *who* they were, often far more than *what* they taught us.[36]

While visiting friends, we met one of my former English students in the countryside. Eleven years previously, she had been in her teens and one of the brightest students in my beginners' class. Not long after passing my class with flying colours, she had come to faith and experienced strong family opposition. All these years later, she had married a church leader and cradled a baby. On the off-chance, she

---

36. The so-called 'observer's paradox' was a constant encouragement because the simple presence of the teacher has influence and impact in and out of the classroom.

happened to mention the first person who shared the Good News with her. It was someone who I would never guess: myself. I was dumbstruck because I had no recollection of talking to her about it. I hardly spoke any Lao at the time and she had just started learning English.

Removing rocks, sowing seeds, pointing to the good, and awakening thirst were all pointers to the kingdom. The wind blew where it wanted. This was and continues to be His work and He knows the hearts of all. The amazing thing was that He asked us to partner with Him. Even without us knowing anything about it.[37] Rather than seeing 'outreach' as doing something else supposedly more spiritual once teaching was out of the way, we were convinced that teaching was *the* outreach or at least a significant part of witness to Him.

---

37. The turning of thousands of the Hmong people to Christ in Xieng Khouang province in northern Laos happened when those sharing the gospel were not even there. See Adrianoff, Jean., *Chosen for a Special Joy: The Story of Ted and Ruth Adrianoff* (Chicago: Wingspread Publishers, 2001).

Chapter 8 – The Seen and the Unseen

You did not have to be in Laos all that long before you started receiving wedding invitations from colleagues, neighbours, and even people you did not know at all. This was the chance to dress up in your finery and plunge into Lao culture. Invitations came in the form of an envelope with the recipient's name printed on the outside and a card inside bearing the names of the folk getting married along with the location and timing.

In the evening after the wedding, food was usually provided at the restaurant in the form of a self-service buffet. When the signal was given to go and get your food, it was astounding how the gentle, gracious Lao were instantaneously transformed into a shoving, elbowing mob in the rush to get to the food.

The first time we went to a wedding dinner in the evening, we conspired to use our own unmarked envelope for our cash gift and placed it directly in the bride's hands. If she was surprised at our barbaric ways, she did not show it, accepting our gift with a gracious smile. Little did we know that the gigantic, unmissable box at the entrance was for dropping in our cash gift envelope with our pre-printed names on. This system, of course, enabled the essential task later on of working out who gave what.

It was fairly important to know whose wedding it was that you were invited to and where it was being held. This was made all the more interesting in that invitations and all-important information were printed nearly entirely in Lao. Some friends of ours dutifully dropped their cash-gift envelope in the appropriate box, and munched their way through copious amounts of food before realising that the wedding they had been invited to was in fact in the adjacent venue.

On the wedding day, an all-important *baci*[38] ceremony would be held in the morning, one of *the* hallmarks of Lao society. This stemmed from the belief that we are a collection of thirty-two organs, each having its own spirit to protect it. At times of change such as sickness, loss, celebration, and travel, these spirits had a tendency to wander outside the body causing imbalance, upset, and misfortune. The tying of white strings onto the wrists of the people involved reconnected the spirits to the body bringing wholeness, health, harmony, and wellbeing.

Apart from having tremendous social significance, the ceremony was also an intensely religious time involving Buddhist rituals and an invitation for the spirits to come. Monks were usually present with chanting in Pali. It was also a powerful and beautiful time when relationships within the family and the whole community were acknowledged, reaffirmed, and strengthened. The person or people in need of wholeness could be assured that everyone was by their side.

We were conscious that refraining from string-tying was a 'marker' of a Christian as seen by the main local church body, the Lao Evangelical Church (LEC). Along with alcohol, the issue of string-tying was contentious and people often asked us what we thought. We had to be very diplomatic and careful with our answers. The last thing we wanted was to hurt, confuse, and alienate other Christians and newcomers to the faith. At the same time, we heard amazing testimonies of how string-tying in the name of Jesus had been a powerful cultural witness.[39] We would often quietly and gently point to our freedom in Christ. Yet having the love to curtail that freedom in consideration for others and

---

38. Also known as '*Sou Khuan*' (spirit calling), the *baci* ceremony looked like Buddhism but was animism at heart.
39. Christ was present and active in culture when those from Buddhist backgrounds used string-tying, a cross, and prayers in the name of Jesus to minister to the sick and elderly. For similar stories see Fucella, *Behind the Smiles: Tales from Life in Thailand*, p.71-72.

the wider situation was also Christ-like.[40]

String-tying symbolised a yearning for wholeness, something we also longed to see for the Buddhist people in front of us. We needed to show Christ's love by being willing to find ways of connecting with the things that were very important to Lao people. We encouraged our Lao friends to find ways of revering Christ as Lord in the midst of Buddhist culture and everyday activities. I often think of the young Christian who had to bury his father along with Buddhist rites. His mind was fixed on Jesus during a horrendously upsetting and difficult time. Would it have helped demonstrate Christ's love if he had refused to participate with the entire community present?

As for us, we decided to walk the middle road of showing respect and love for the Lao people and their ways of doing things but not actually participating in the string-tying itself. We made sure we were quietly present, supportive, and gave gifts in the expected way. We never sensed any hurt or offence. The graciousness of local people in these situations never ceased to amaze us.

From the start of our time in Laos, we had been drawn to the southern province of Savannakhet. An awareness, a fascination, a burden to pray and be poised to respond. By 2017, we had been leading the English Centre for a few years, relishing the interaction and opportunities for witness it enabled with people from all walks of life.

Imagine our shock when a complete stranger prayed with me and shared afterwards how he felt God saying that I was reading a book but was unable to turn the pages. There was no need to fear, however, because God Himself would turn the pages to the next chapter.

---

40. Christians through the ages have wrestled with these issues: being free in Christ but not ever wanting to be a 'stumbling block' to others (see 1 Corinthians 8).

Around the same time, another person prayed for Mei and shared how she would soon experience a shaking in her life. It was a shaking, however, of an entirely good kind. How unsettling, exciting, encouraging, and nerve-racking.[41]

When an English Centre finally opened there in 2017, we jumped at the chance to get involved. The road was before us but it was still painful to walk on it. Many tears were shed as we wrestled with the decision. Once again, our lives were placed into His hands as we moved away from all the relationships and inroads everyone in our family had built up over many years in the capital.

We relished our roles working alongside the expat teachers and local staff at the English Centre in Vientiane. The children were happy and settled with their school, friends, and routines. Although Keziah was finishing primary school, there was the option of continuing into middle school. Many of her teachers were Christians we trusted and appreciated. There were also the local and expat fellowships with the presence of several 'old-timers' who often had timely and powerful 'words in season' for us. There were hardly any expats in Savannakhet let alone an expat fellowship. Would we even be allowed to attend local church?

Although miraculously, there was an English-medium school in Savannakhet; it had only just opened with limited classes. Mei and I agreed that if there was a class for Keziah, this would be a sign we were meant to go. One of the first encouragements was calling up the school and confirming that there would be a class for Keziah.

The new English Centre needed help to get started and I drove down a group of teachers. It was also a great opportunity to visit the international school. The soothing family atmosphere and environment of the tropical gardens and spacious play areas were striking. In these

---

41. In seeking God's guidance for the work and our lives, we regularly prayed with and sought the advice of mature Christians. There was often a certain, terrible vulnerability in doing so. Hearing from God caused us to tremble! (See Isaiah 66:2.)

comforting details, I was reminded that Father God specialised in giving good gifts.[42]

It was time to hunt for a suitable house to rent. Without housing agents or internet ads, the only approach was to drive the seven hours there, ask around, and scan the streets for *huan hai sao* (house for rent) signs. A fantastic way of getting to know people and the surroundings if not all that efficient. Our first trip down was completely unsuccessful and we returned to Vientiane rather crestfallen.

At the next opportunity, we again drove down. We passed by a large, tumbledown house in an overrun tropical garden. There was no *huan hai sao* sign. The front gate slid open and looking inside, we were greeted with a hearty '*Sabaidee*' from a tall, gaunt, ageing man. Yes, the house was for rent. It was late in the day and the children were fed-up with the housing search. At this house, however, both were keen to get out of the car and take a look.

A steep-sided pond topped with luminous algae backed on to the house. For people who could afford it, ponds were dug out near to or even beneath houses and served as a fish market, fridge, and relaxation spot. Thankfully for us in terms of safety and privacy, this pond was walled and gated off. Not only were ponds hazardous if a person or animal slipped in but were a breeding ground for mosquitoes if fish were not kept.

It suddenly dawned on us that the elderly man was not the landlord but was keeping an eye on the place. He readily agreed to open up the house. It seemed perfect for us even if mental alarm bells were going off at the large expanse of waist-high grass surrounding it. When it was time to leave and see if there were any other houses for rent, I asked for a cutting of the magnificent *dok champa* flowers (frangipani) dotting the

---

42. We were constantly astounded by how God constantly worked beauty into the details. Ultimately, the gifts of life, a new day, the kindness of strangers, a sunset, or the wonderful smell of tropical rain on cement were all from Him (see Matthew 7:9-11).

garden. They were a stunning burgundy rather than the usual white. We need not have taken it as soon afterwards we decided to rent that house. It was clearly another wonderful provision from Him.

View from Savannakhet across the Mekong River to Mukdahan on the Thai side

It was time to move house from Vientiane to the south. We packed our little car to the brim with more stuff strapped to the roof and made the long journey along with our cat, two guinea pigs, and two rabbits. The journey went exceptionally well except Mei having to brave the last few hours with damp jeans from a certain warm discharge from the rabbit cage.

Over the months that followed, I sought out openings to spend time with the elderly man and his family, who happened to be our neighbours on the other side of the pond. We helped one another and got to have exchanges on issues of food, family, work, and faith.

Fast forward six months. We needed to make a journey out of town and I popped around to ask if our neighbour could stay over and guard the house as he had done so on numerous occasions. He looked exhausted and said he was tired and could not help. This was concerning. On returning from our trip, I went to check on his well-being. I was glad that a wise, older friend accompanied me. He just happened to be staying with us and had lived in the country for ten years before the regime change in 1975.

As we neared the house, one of our neighbour's daughters called out to us that her father was very sick. Even so, the sight of his rapid deterioration was heart-breaking. The entire family were present. Not a good sign. After graciously being granted permission to pray in the local language to the 'Lord God who created everything', our neighbour mustered enough energy to put his hands together and say thank you.

The next morning, I was out in the garden. From the rustling on the other side of the fence, I knew that one of the neighbours was making her way through the undergrowth. She called out to me that her father had passed away in the night. In our sorrow, we could only commit him to His compassion and mercy.

However, I was aware that we had prayed for someone in the presence of others and that person had died. What would the family and all the onlookers think of that? Would careless chatter or even accusation turn our intentions of care and concern into something more sinister, evil, and dangerous? We had experienced how prayer often led into an arena, a real physical and spiritual conflict, where situations and relationships could suddenly turn for the worse or be miraculously impacted for the better in an instant.

Mustering up courage, I walked round to our neighbour's home the next day to pay my respects. Would I be welcome? There were a few people outside the house eating and drinking under canopies that were rented for the occasion. Hardly anyone even glanced in my direction. More folks were sitting quietly on the floor inside, facing towards the coffin. They gently beckoned for me to enter. The coffin was decorated with fairy lights, a framed photograph placed before it, Buddhist symbols placed around it. The photo showed a man proud and handsome in his younger days. There were incense sticks to burn, money to place in a bowl, Buddhist chants and prayers to be said. Respectful and appropriate action was called for in the midst of a delicate situation.

It was then that I spotted our landlady sitting nearby. Breathing a prayer of thanks, I quietly asked her advice on how best to pay my respects. Her reply in Lao was gentle and wise: 'Just go forward to the coffin and say out loud your thankfulness for his life and put your gift in the basket.' With head lowered, I did just that. A prayer to Him of gratefulness for the brief time experienced with our neighbour. An expression of wonder at how meaningful the Buddhist ways of doing things were in that moment. A prayer that He would protect us and preserve the relationship with the family and community.

The passing away of our neighbour unleashed troubling issues which perhaps were lurking under the surface the whole time. One of his sons often climbed over our low-lying spike-topped fence and strolled around the garden to gather fruit, edible leaves, and hordes of red ants in the mango trees. Ant egg soup was a particular favourite. It was clear that he had always done this. I was glad to let him take as much as he wanted, which usually amounted to two or three huge bags full of insects, seeds, plants, and fruit.

My heart went out to him. He was clearly mentally unstable, dishevelled, and as thin as anything. Moreover, his father was a good man who had helped us out graciously and with faithfulness. The foraging also assisted with the impossible task of keeping down the relentless advance of the tropical undergrowth. By the time he had finished clambering around the trees, furious red ants were crawling all over his hair and face. He did not seem to mind them at all.

I tried to reach out to him in compassion, offering him small gardening jobs which he eagerly accepted for cash. There was one day where he refused to go home until every leaf was brushed up and every blade of grass was poked out of the cracks in the cement. How thorough and what a great attitude. If only more people were like this, the world would be a better place.

Coming in unannounced, however, left us feeling ill at ease. I asked him to stop clambering over the wall but enter through the gate at the front of the house like everyone else. One of the most challenging things in Laos was constantly having to balance reaching out in Christ-like compassion, forgiveness, and patience yet not encouraging behaviour that local people, let alone foreigners, would see as definitely crossing the line.

Nearly everyone in Laos left their front gates unlocked in the day, although security was guaranteed through the household dogs and Grandma who was usually permanently deployed to keep a beady eye on everything. Although we never kept dogs, having an unlocked gate was part of our pro-active approach to showing openness, trust, welcome, and availability.

Thankfully, our neighbour understood what I was trying to get him to do and he started calling through the fence for permission to come in and gather food. All of us were safer for knowing where he was. However, I took care to remind Mei to start locking the gate and front door whenever I went into town.

Shortly afterwards, during a thunderstorm, one of our cats went missing. After hunting far and wide and getting to know all the neighbours by going house-to-house to ask if they had seen it, we had to give it up as gone. Could our unstable neighbour have had something to do with it? There was no way of knowing. Our policeman neighbour certainly thought so when he indicated the shack with a dismissive wave of his hand: 'He's crazy and takes drugs.'

The neighbours probably thought I was a bit loopy caring so much about a cat, but it was touching when one lady around the back actually made the effort to call a few days later with a description of a cat they had seen although it was not the right one.

In Lao language, *yaba*, the word for amphetamines, literally translated as 'crazy drug', an all-too-accurate description. They were cheap, easy to find, and supposedly staved off hunger for days. A friend who led up a drug rehabilitation centre for years in Vientiane shared with me that most of the young men under his care hailed from Savannakhet.

On our first day in the house we had just rented in Savannakhet, one of the young men from his centre popped round to visit us. It was a lovely gesture seeing as he only had a few days' leave from the Vientiane rehab centre to visit his family. The first thing he did was to warn us to be very careful as 'bad people doing drugs' lived round the back. He should know. What an ominous start to our new life in the south.

The following summer while we were away in the UK, the people who had agreed to look after our house left a disturbing message on my phone describing how someone kept on climbing over the wall and was getting the fruit down from the trees. It must have been our unstable neighbour. What a fright for our house-sitters to suddenly encounter a wild-looking stranger high up in the trees right in front of them. On top of that, silly little items started growing legs such as a school *sinh* (Lao-style skirt) and a large water storage bottle. Things of little consequence except for a violation of neighbourly trust, security, and peace. Our house-sitters were students in my English class, young girls in their early twenties, not really ideal candidates for a confrontation with a potentially drugged-up male intruder.

I got in touch with the landlady from the UK (the power and ease of modern technology), and she agreed to shore up the fencing at the back of the house. A few days later, a nice photo of the finished job sat on my phone and a recorded message of thanks in Lao was conveyed back in return. Surely the raised fencing with customary barbed wire would discourage our neighbour and add a sense of security for our house-sitters and ourselves when we returned.

The very next day, our distraught house-sitters got in touch to say that someone had climbed in during the night and taken our rabbits from their cage outside, much to the consternation of our kids. They had reared them since small. Was it some sort of angry indignation on the part of our neighbour at being prevented from entering a place he saw as rightfully his? Was it provocation as if a mere fence could stop him? Or was it drug-induced madness, readily forgotten the next day? Or was it all sheer coincidence involving someone else altogether? The uneasiness was heavy. There was nothing more our landlady could do and we were due to return anyway.

Over the next year, we lost two further cats. We suspected our neighbour had something to do with it but had no proof except to witness his mental deterioration, often involving muttering to himself and frequently breaking out into a loud, screechy female voice. This eerie sound was extremely disconcerting and not something you could ever get used to. Remembering the lordship of Jesus was so difficult in these uneasy moments as we realised that the demonic was intertwined with his destitution, addiction, rejection from society, and mental state. Was it worth continuing to live there? Should we give up and move out or continue in patience and love?

Then one day, we heard the awful sound of smashing glass. On rushing outside, we were greeted with shattered glass all over the cement from a beer bottle which had come over the wall near to where the children played. The landlady was duly informed and promised to have a word with the neighbour in the most appropriate way possible in Laos: through the network and influence of the family, community, and village leaders.

All was peaceful until a few weeks later. Loud crashing sounds started coming from outside. At first, I assumed it was the children making the racket but when I shouted and got no response, I rushed outside. Puzzled, I saw pebbles on the ground and the chatter of birds overhead. I remember thinking whether it was possible for birds to pick up stones and drop them in flight. I grabbed a chair and peered over the wall at each of the neighbouring houses. There was not a soul. No one at all.

Then in the corner of my eye, I spied a window shutter on our neighbour's house opening just a crack and swiftly closing again. To my disbelief, a slingshot appeared followed by a volley of pebbles. Instinctively, I ducked and sheltered my eyes. I shouted for him to stop! It was dangerous! To which he replied that he could do what he liked.

I yelled to the girls to grab the cats and rush inside for we were in danger of losing an eye or being showered with glass if a window caved in. Our car was directly in the firing line. Grabbing the car keys, I reversed it speedily to the other side of the house. Later, Mei noticed that a pane of glass in our youngest daughter's bedroom window had shattered, but apart from that, we were shaken but fine.

When the incident was reported to our landlady, she was sympathetic but patiently reminded us that no self-respecting village headman would do anything. Unless we had a video. What a perfect response to a tricky community problem. She did offer to install cameras but to what purpose? Our Christian witness just could not fathom our neighbour being carted off to a pitiless prison to most likely spend the rest of his days there. At the same time, our peace had literally been shattered, every little noise made us anxious, and we kept away from the back of the house in case something suddenly flew over the wall. Just a few days later, in fact, more bottles flew over and smashed to smithereens.

Incredibly after all of this, I felt strangely convicted. I had responded to the madness by doing the most logical thing: cutting off our neighbour and building ever-higher mental and physical walls. Against all my intuition, I resolved to pray for and bless my neighbour by making sure that he was fed through the week. My mother had told me that some people in England fed foxes to prevent them coming after their cats. Perhaps extreme hunger was one of the causes of our neighbour's behaviour. I started to pick up the kind of meat snacks, instant noodles, and porridge that all local people loved and dropped them off outside his house. Perhaps a full stomach would calm his temperament, reduce the desperation and nuisance-making hyperactivity of whatever he had been taking, and remind him we cared for him.

It seemed to work! Peace was restored although our hearts beat a little faster whenever we saw our neighbour in the no-man's land straddling the back of our garden wall. Often, he would just sit on the wall for hours staring at us. When I decided to bring him food, the first thing I did was to ask him his name. I wanted to remind myself of his dignity, a created being.

One day, as I was attending to some chores in the house, I heard our neighbour's all-too-familiar screechy rant and strangely welcomed it. Rushing out with some milk and fruit, I saw him squatting on top of the wall outside his house, lost to the world, shrieking literally like a man possessed. Calling out his name, it was remarkable to see an immediate physical change, a quiet, calm man looking expectantly at me. He readily accepted my care package with a *kop jai* (thank you) in the politest local way possible before disappearing once again over his wall. Never forget the power of names.

In 2020, during the Lao New Year festivities, the country had descended into lockdown due to the havoc wreaked by COVID. I was working on my computer when Kaelyn came in and told me as instructed that 'the neighbour was there'. Rushing downstairs, I gathered up some food items and seeing him peering through the fence, went over to greet him. Sticking the items through the chain-link fence, I retreated a couple of metres as per COVID guidance, waiting for him to retrieve them. Instead, he motioned to me to come forward and hold out my hands, palms open. I did so with heart thumping. He then proceeded to pour 'holy water' filled with fragrant flowers over my hands through the fence. This was a Buddhist New Year blessing, only really carried out by children for their parents or elders. Although my mind was full of thoughts of COVID, it was an incredibly surreal and moving gesture. If we could see our lives from His perspective, I suspect we would be dumbfounded at how our lives, presence, words, and actions impacted others both in the seen and the unseen.

Chapter 9 – Same, Same But Different

Our beloved country of Laos has changed incredibly since we first arrived in 2008. Nevertheless, Vientiane remains Asia's most laid-back capital with the most delicate skyline. For years, only one building was permitted to eclipse *That Luang* stupa[43], the most revered Buddhist site in the country. In recent years, clusters of glass and cement towers earmarked for banks, offices, and apartments have started popping up everywhere in this overgrown town-of-a-city.

In the countryside, massive appropriation of land, huge dams, and hydroelectric plants have displaced countless villages and farmlands forever, together with the waterflow and fish stocks of the Mekong and other rivers.[44] Many species of animals unique to Laos such as the Asian unicorn, the *saola*,[45] are critically endangered. A contentious Chinese-built railway line through formidable mountain ranges from Kunming to the Lao capital is operational. As huge trucks thunder through the narrow Lao roads to and from Yunnan, Danang, and Thailand, it is all too easy to think about Laos not on its own terms but from the impact of the powerful countries surrounding it.[46] Yet with all these changes and pressures, local people, for the most part, still exude grace, patience, and welcome.

---

43. A stupa is a moundlike structure containing relics typically the remains of a revered monk or nun.

44. In a developing country snaked with rivers and few energy sources, foreign exchange is generated through hydropower which is sold to Thailand. Although damaging to communities and the environment, it is difficult to see viable alternatives for the Lao government (see Osborne, *The Mekong: Turbulent Past, Uncertain Future*, pp. 241-246).

45. The mysterious and elusive *saola* are cousins of cattle and resemble antelopes. For a beautiful, richly descriptive account of the *saola* in the jungles of Laos see William deBuys, *The Last Unicorn: A Search for One of Earth's Rarest Creatures* (Kindle, Little, Brown & Company, 2015).

46. At least this writer acknowledges the flawed task of writing about other people's nations and cultures (see Holt, *Spirits of the Place: Buddhism and Lao Religious Culture*), p.1.

In recent years, Laos has become much more 'land-linked' than land-locked.[47] Yet after all these years with many countries jostling for influence, most people still seem to look to Thailand for just about everything. Once-sleepy towns on both sides of the Mekong have become plump on Lao-driven commerce. With linguistic, religious, and cultural similarities, Thai companies and chains have had arguably the most success in Laos. The sticky rice-eating, *padek*-loving, *sinh*-wearing, *khen*-playing north-eastern region of Isaan in Thailand shares a lot of Lao cultural markers.[48]

Tranquil marshland in Vientiane earmarked for massive development

It was refreshing not to be inundated with brands and chains in Laos, if rather inconvenient. Most shopping still involved multiple trips to

---

47. I found this the optimistic view (see Evans, *A Short History of Laos: The Land In Between*, p.229). Being land-linked was beneficial to Laos but enabled powerful surrounding countries to become even more influential and assertive.

48. The *khen* is a traditional Lao reed instrument with a striking, haunting sound.

buy individual items at roadside stalls, markets, and minimarts. An altogether time-consuming but wonderful way to get to know people and places. Yet this too has changed with the gradual arrival of vast shopping malls and larger convenience stalls.

Getting around the cities was always a major challenge. Although Japan gifted a fleet of buses in recent years, Vientiane still lacks a reliable public transport system. If unable to borrow a motorbike, people use *tuk-tuks, jumbos,* and *sawntaeos,* with taxis increasingly common. Finding such vehicles, however, entailed a trek to the main road and they were seldom around at meal times or after dark. Although handy for groups or when your mode of transport broke down, costs quickly mounted up if relied upon all the time. That is why almost everyone in Laos purchased a motorbike, a more-or-less essential in grid-locked Vientiane and other cities.

The most common request we experienced at the English Centre was a loan for local staff to buy a motorbike. It was an attractive option as the loan was interest-free and the cost would be gradually deducted from each month's salary. It meant that people ended up earning very little each month, not counting the sparkling new Honda sitting outside. Policies gauging the necessity of loans together with a cap on the amount requested did not really facilitate discussion about financial planning, societal and peer pressure, identity and worth. We saw how the power of advertising to sell instant needs-satisfaction through tempting financing plans resulted in countless people finding themselves under crushing debt.

Although urban centres retained many pockets of slow-moving, old-world charm, we witnessed the relentless onward march of cement and traffic. Many foreigners would not be able to imagine a Laos in 2008 when vehicles were limited to a few vastly overpriced and ageing Japanese pickup trucks or tiny, unreliable Chinese cars. All with an additional 100 per cent tax added in. Thanks to the ingenuity of the Koreans, the roads in recent years were crammed with 'affordable', medium-sized cars. The showrooms which once displayed motorbikes sell cars.

Splashing out on a vehicle in 2008 was too much of a distraction to our desire of living simply. Ten years later, second-hand vehicles were available across the price range. Finding one that did not need significant repairs, however, remained a near-impossible task. As the Koreans move on to more lucrative markets, will car ownership and traffic jams level off?

The tremendous growth in vehicles on the roads meant service stations could be found more or less everywhere. Not too long ago, long journeys with a young child along the Route 13 north-south highway used to involve knocking on random houses by the road asking to use the not-so-public conveniences. What a unique way of meeting and practising Lao with people from all walks of life. Numerous soft toys were waylaid in this manner up and down the country when they were put down by our child only to be forgotten once business was concluded.

With the delight of service stations, there were different toilet types and sometimes even disabled facilities complete with ramp. With some luck, there would be dedicated bins with recycling options, an air-conditioned minimart, a trendy café chain with tempting cakes, and pop-up food stalls. All unthinkable a few years ago.

Many service stations in the countryside, however, had the infrastructure yet nothing at all in the buildings: no water from the taps, nothing for sale, and worse of all no fuel. Always a little anxiety-inducing when the fuel gauge was near-empty in the middle of nowhere. With a little caution, however, the days were gone of having to lug along a spare canister of fuel together with a packed lunch of favourite sandwiches for the journey.

During one long journey, our eldest daughter, Keziah, was distraught when she discovered that she had forgotten her camera in the toilet of a service station. Mei prayed with her that the camera would be found on our return. When we rolled up to the service station the following day, the lady from the shop ran out miraculously waving a familiar item. What a lovely and unlikely answer to a child's prayer.

The flipside of being land-linked is that if the borders were to shut for any length of time there would be instantaneous pandemonium on the Lao side. This was at its clearest during the first COVID lockdown in 2020 when borders closed and a whole host of items such as tinned goods, tofu (vital for the one vegetarian in our family), milk, and bread vanished overnight until goods-only agents were allowed in later. False reports began circling online about Vietnamese fuel stuck at the border causing bedlam at Lao petrol stations. The availability, appeal, and affordability of technology and the internet has resulted in a lot of both useful and questionable information, together with a voracious appetite to attain material goods and live out a certain lifestyle.

When we were gifted our first smartphone in 2009, we were a little shy as we were working with people with little means. In recent times, it seemed like everyone in Laos had *at least* one smartphone. That did not mean people had any credit to actually call anyone or use the internet. That was not the point. Phone ownership underlined a certain status in life. We often found that the only way to remain in contact was to ask people to call us, hang up, and then we would call them back.

Tapping into this scenario, Lao phone companies were forever handing out free SIM cards with a small amount of credit which meant people constantly changed their numbers. We found ourselves continually having to chase up friends' new numbers with the high risk of losing contact altogether as their credit ran out. Our phone contacts were full of names followed by lists of all the various numbers they may have been using.

We found that many of our local friends preferred data SIMs which were entirely for internet use with no number for direct calls. The issue was that people assumed everyone had data on their phone at all times. Great for light-hearted connections on social media but not so good for last-minute arrangements and work commitments. Moreover, if people ran out of credit, there really was no way to contact them outside of the internet. It was often easier to jump on a motorbike and ride over to the person's house to relay the message in person.

Phones were so common that they rapidly became annoying. Any sort of swimming in Laos needed to be accompanied by ear-splitting techno from a suitcase-sized portable speaker connected to someone's phone. True to form, this racket would always be interrupted after a few seconds by an incoming call, the ring tune magnified a thousand times for all present to savour.

One of our neighbours discovered the joys of playing the radio from his phone through giant speakers for the entire community to enjoy. No complaining to the police about noise pollution. He was the police and quite a gruff one at that. Apart from having to endure the constant crackling of the poor connection, he chose a radio station that played traditional Lao music which actually became quite enjoyable to hum along to. It was amazing the things you could get used to if they were accepted as the way things were. We did not know whether to laugh or cry, however, when he discovered that a nifty way of calming his baby was to play 'Incey Wincey Spider' in English on repeat for hours on end.

It was clear that purchasing power and disposable income had become all the more apparent. Yet what did this mean for the have-nots? The gap between the poor and everyone else had become ever-wider and much more in-your-face. Our neighbours would often spend evenings maintaining their motorbikes. In recent years, they moved on to fitting massive speakers with flashing lights into the boots of sleek-looking cars. I was so nervous the glass in our windows would shatter every time they tested out the thumping bass.

Our hearts went out to the mentally unstable who were always walking, always on the move, continuously ambling up and down the roads in the heat of the day. No peace, no rest, a restlessness, a weariness. Some would be in a state of undress and motorists would tease and film them on their mobile phones, sharing the images with all their friends. The local people we mentioned this to thought nothing of it. Christians shrugged their shoulders. There did not seem to be anyone who recognised the issue for what it was. Perhaps refusing to see the issue meant it somehow did not exist? The only 'help' we saw was when unstable people were chained to the wall of their house or taken away goodness knows where.

The memory of an unstable lady with a listless infant on her shoulder will forever be etched on our minds. We first saw her wandering aimlessly around in the searing heat as we were buying fruit nearby. Seeing the state of the child and fearing for its life, we offered her oranges. Perhaps the juice and vitamins would help. In her insanity, she refused and walked off. Days later, we saw a group of men, perhaps militia sent from the village leader, haul her away by a chain. Alone.

We always collected clothes for the poor and unstable. It was the least we could do. Mei offered a bag of suitable clothing to one lady who we had spotted wandering up and down the streets. Instead of taking the bag and shuffling off, she rifled through the clothes and chose the items that she liked best, returning the rest to Mei. We were reminded that people even in the direst circumstances had a right to retain their dignity, their humanity. The freedom to choose was part of this.

In Savannakhet, a wild-looking, dishevelled man with no legs would drag himself along with his hands every day in the middle of the main shopping street, the traffic at a standstill. I longed to help but had no idea how. Everyone avoided him. This was understandable as he was entirely unpredictable and would often burst out screaming. Would he lash out and attack? People we talked to always said the same thing: 'He has a family', 'He lives in a house over there', 'He's not a good person.' The demonic, the trauma of his mutilation, rejection, poverty, insanity. We could brainstorm all the possible frightening factors but in the name of Christ, I held out bananas and a chilled bottle of water. He grabbed and wolfed them down. On another occasion he entirely ignored the *khao jee pate*[49] I held out to him and shuffled on by. The helplessness of the situation was deeply unsettling.

In all the locations we lived, we noticed folk scavenging through the rubbish for plastic bottles to earn a pittance by selling them for recycling. We always saved our plastic bottles in large bags which we stored at the back of our car and offered them to anyone we spotted collecting. We fondly remember the cheerful husband and wife team pulling their cart filled with bottles through the streets with their lovely children sitting on top. Although their lives must have been dreadfully hard, their weary faces always had huge smiles and a hearty *'Sabaidee'*. Our hearts melted as the children hugged the soft toys and clothes we had saved for them.

When we first arrived in Laos, there were hardly any beggars amidst stories that the police kept a strict eye and carted them away to prison islands in the middle of a vast lake. Over the years, this policy was clearly relaxed. We were dazed and heartbroken by rows of men lying prostrate before the hordes of passers-by and tourists in the main thoroughfare of the Vientiane night market. It was horrifying to witness such self-abasement and desperation.

In the unforgiving heat and dust, cold water was incredibly appreciated by tired, thirsty, needy people. We started purchasing crates of bottled water and chilling a few bottles overnight in the fridge. The next day, we would hand them out to anyone who looked like they could do with

---

49. Delicious, French-legacy baguette adored by all in Laos, filled with pâté, meat, salad, with lashings of mayo and chili sauce.

one: the dignified, elderly lady taking a breather on the shop steps after a long walk; the sweating labourers digging up the road in the hot sun; the weary, middle-aged couple walking to the bus station after a check-up at the hospital; the dishevelled beggars and their bright-eyed children; the unstable people walking up and down with their uncomprehending stares. Perhaps they also needed someone to *see* them, to talk to them, to shine a ray of Christ-like goodness in their lives, even for a moment.

We were a little sceptical when local people told us about the 'professional begging villages' but we soon started noticing the same shabby-looking women and children with tell-tale begging bowls tramping along the side of the roads. Our hearts went out to the children who were dressed in rags and should have been in school or a loving home. We often handed out bottles of chilled water, toys, and a few notes. The aggression of the women, however, was astonishing. Whatever we gave, it was never enough and they would start shouting and yelling, pulling at our clothes and making a scene.

After giving one small girl a soft toy, we gulped in dismay as the woman in charge of her clouted her around the head and grabbed the toy. Our hearts broke at the child's tears but we were relieved when the toy was given back. It was not money. The situation was tragic. How we longed to gather up the children and give them a safe place to live.

Whatever the rights and wrongs, the pros and cons of getting involved, we always found it very difficult in our abundance to pass the needy without doing something, even if it meant simply noticing, saying a quiet prayer, and pausing for a moment to offer a gentle *Sabaidee*.

Without a doubt, the time of year that we most anticipated was Christmas as it was the *only* time in Laos that Christians could share more openly about their faith. In any other context, even a mention of Christianity would likely be met with a grim, stony silence at best and persecution, shame, and suffering at worst. Globalisation has hugely assisted Christmas becoming more noticed, more tolerated, and even 'celebrated' in Laos. Well before December, Santa hats, plastic trees, fairy lights, and tinsel started popping up in shops and markets in the cities. Even so, one market-stall holder in Savannakhet informed me that such decorations were only 'for the Christians'.

In a curious local twist, one Christmas non-negotiable in Laos was the gift exchange. A Lao Christmas seemed to be incomplete without one and most workplaces, churches, and even government offices organised one. Well before the exchange, people got all hot under the collar discussing the budget for gifts and how and when items were to be dispersed. To pick out a gift and present it to someone was almost akin to a sacred act for many people we met. There was a tremendous potential for loss of face if the gift was ignored, scorned, seen to be stingy or somehow not good enough. Some foreigners introduced a 'stealing' element to the exchange which could be great fun but sometimes went against the spirit of the occasion from a local point of view. Nevertheless, folks rarely let on that they were in any way aggrieved. As experts in anticipating and navigating potentially unsettling experiences, smiles and even laughter were employed to maintain an easy-going camaraderie and social cohesion.

Having International New Year just around the corner to Christmas has certainly helped local people accept such foreign eccentricities. In many local minds, the two celebrations were probably one and the same thing. The 'cow-down' (countdown) just before midnight on New Year's Eve was made all the more fun because curiously, it was only done in English and people often forgot what the next numbers were to howls of raucous and often alcohol-fuelled laughter.

The global Church should take a leaf out of Laos' book because Christmas was not merely celebrated over two or three days but *every* day of December and often well into January. How long this will be tolerated at an official level remains to be seen but every church in each province is allocated their own day to celebrate and everyone attends each other's services. These invariably went on all day and well into the night with street-side Christian films and refreshments.

For those mostly urban churches that could afford it, an additional evening service was put on in the week, a chance for the children and teens to show off their latest Korean dance moves. Government officials and even members of the police were invited (often in full uniform) and presented with wonderfully wrapped gifts before everyone sat down to a sumptuous feast afterwards. When you only get one occasion a year to celebrate your faith, why do things by half?

It was often hard for the smaller, rural churches to keep up with all these well-intentioned goings-on. We had been attending a small, humble church outside Pakse and the leaders had excitedly committed themselves to putting on an ambitious Christmas programme with prominent members of the government as guests. We offered to assist by getting some paint to spruce up the tired-looking meeting room. Imagine two cows and a puppy sauntering down the aisle as the youth turned up to get to work on the walls. We used huge banana tree leaves to protect the floor but there were still splodges of paint all over jeans and skirts. No one seemed to mind and it was a great time of joy and unity as people worked together.

Our Christmas event was the only real chance in the year to share a little more about the festival with our students. The creativity was in sharing in sensitive and respectful ways that Lao people could relate to and understand without feeling in any way intimidated or pressured. The staff sang some popular and traditional Christmas songs and carols and taught the meaning behind some of the vocabulary. We also talked about some common Christmas symbols such as the tree, bell, and star, and prepared a brief explanation in Lao and English about the meanings within the Christmas context. The bell, for instance, was a symbol of good news. Apart from presents and togetherness at Christmas, what was this good news? Only when people asked, did we explain a little more.

Another approach was through making 'Christingles' using oranges, candles, red ribbon, raisins, and toothpicks. We modified and softened the story behind 'the Christingle' to better suit Lao sensitivities. It went something like this. It was Christmas time in the Czech Republic and the leader of a church asked all the children to bring a gift to give to Jesus. One family of three children were very poor and the only thing they had was an orange. The top was rotten so one of the children cut out the bad part and stuck a candle in the hole. To make it look more presentable, another child took her red ribbon from her hair and attached it around the middle of the orange using toothpicks. The third child stuck raisins on the ends of the sticks.

They took it to church and the other children made fun of their gift. However, the leader of the church took it and told everyone that it was very special because it showed the meaning of Christmas for the following reasons: the orange is the world; the candle gives light in the darkness like God's love; the four sticks point in all directions and symbolise north, south, east and west and all the people in the world; the red ribbon symbolises how Jesus died for the bad things we have done; the raisins tell of the good things that God gives to everyone.

One of our students decided to use sticky rice instead of the raisins on the tooth picks. How fitting as all Lao people love sticky rice and everyone present recognised it as a unique and wonderful blessing in their nation.

The students were very taken with the craft and story and it was lovely to discuss the meaning of Christmas while sitting, eating, and taking photos in the warm glow of candles. People from Buddhist backgrounds love candles and bright colours such as orange and red. Everyone loves selfies, delicious food, and togetherness.

On more than one occasion, it started raining heavily just before students were due to arrive for the Christmas events we put on. Rain was unheard of in December during the dry season. This seemed more than coincidence and we were wary of how evil could bring discouragement in subtle ways to the witness of the activities. Although many were prevented from coming, a few bedraggled students braved the rain on their motorbikes and got to hear more about the meaning of Christmas. The students often had quiet questions and we had opportunities to chat and discuss more with them at a separate time.

Making Christingles

At an Easter-themed student event, we talked about new life followed by egg decorating. As creativity flowed, we asked a few students if they wanted to share with everyone about the designs on their eggs. We were amazed when a Buddhist student eloquently explained the story behind the cross she had chosen to draw on her egg. Her heart had been touched and she would later come to faith even with fierce pressure from her father to change her mind.

At student events, we tried to factor in small group discussion so that opportunities were created for both expat and local Christian staff to interact and hear more from students about their questions, thoughts, and ideas. Refreshments would be served and groups would have discussion questions about the theme of the event which encouraged English practice but also facilitated relationship-building and meaningful conversation.

During one such discussion, an expat English teacher thought she had understood a student sharing with the group about how scared she was of letting her parents know about her new-found faith. After double-checking, it was clear that the student needed the input of someone more experienced in the faith. A local staff member was asked to join the conversation and the student left feeling encouraged and supported, but only after locals and expats had worked together as a team.

Over the years we saw development and progress in certain aspects of Lao society: the new money that flowed from the powerful and influential. We were grateful that through the vehicle of learning English, the privileged could see and hear snippets of good news through the witness of our daily lives. At the same time, we were determined to remember the poor, the rejected, the disabled, the addicts, and the possessed.

We galvanised prayer among colleagues and supporters, and we took some action personally but there was always the feeling that we could have done more. That is why partnership was so important to us: the help of local and international organisations, awareness-raising among the people we knew, and the compassion and love of the Church.

Chapter 10 – Entering Another Black Hole

We love Laos and its people and we could never quite understand how after arriving in such an amazing place, some foreigners would start planning when to leave again. Perhaps to take a holiday, go shopping in Thai malls, or simply to get away. We got used to people not staying in Laos all that long before they moved on. For good.

People often talked about the oppressive atmosphere or 'spiritual heaviness' but we never sensed that. It was always with a sigh of relief whenever we touched back down on Lao soil or crossed the Mekong back into Laos via one of the Friendship bridges. It was with insight that a friend wondered how much of this was because of the persistent, faithful prayers of people from all around the world: upholding, encouraging, and fighting for us.

We are incredibly grateful for the opportunity of bringing up our children in Laos. Living simply, loving others as ourselves, and being deeply aware of community. The freedom of time-slowed-down meant people rather than tasks became the priority and focus. The beauty of the country with its massive skies and wide-open spaces took our breath away time and time again. We loved exploring on foot, by motorbikes and bicycles as a family. We splashed and wallowed in stunning waterfalls, boated into deep caverns, savoured karst mountains under sunsets, and visited people from all walks of life in the villages and cities.

Life was enriching but often far from straightforward. No two days were the same and we loved that. In often unpredictable and sometimes precarious circumstances, we were able to persevere because of His grace and encouragement. Whether it was sticking at learning a language, being treated unfairly, gossiped about, managing unrealistic expectations both from others and ourselves, having regularly disturbed sleep, or contemplating what to do about schooling for the children, we experienced a contentment and joy that was God-given.[50]

There was confidence in the knowledge that He had called us and the necessary resources would be provided. They always were but never in the timing we expected or hoped for. The provision, whether it was a tricky relationship, an answer, job, school, finances, or the way ahead, was often blurry, unseen, and just out of reach. Life was often unsettling and frightening in the unknown of it all. Time and time again, we needed to step out with great courage, faith, and trust that He would hold us.

Living out the life of Proverbs 30:8-9 was a reality for us. Like the writer, we prayed for neither poverty nor riches, but simply what we needed each day. If given too much, we ran the risk of shifting our attention from God to ourselves. If we had too little, on the other hand, we would look at others and be tempted to be bitter and dissatisfied. By doing so, we would dishonour God. In it all, the amazing thing was that we were never in lack. We experienced the greatest gift of all: satisfaction.

In 2019, we started to seriously contemplate the unthinkable thought: God may be moving us on from Laos. My mother had been unwell for a few years and she needed our help and presence. The time had come for us to make a decision. This would not be just for a visit or a holiday. The children loved Laos just as much as we did, with close friends they loved, beloved pets, favourite activities, a house they called home, choice food, and cherished routines. Laos had truly worked its way into our hearts and become home. Amidst the turmoil of our hearts, we had peace as we arrived at the decision together. As a family.

We comforted ourselves by remembering that Keziah's school was not

---

50. Miraculous, persevering, God-given contentment in all circumstances was a powerful encouragement and witness to others (see Philippians 4:11-13, 1 Timothy 6:6-7, 2 Corinthians 12:9-10).

equipped to offer preparation for GCSEs and reliable, qualified teachers were getting increasingly difficult to come by in the south of Laos. We would have had to look for online provision or move to Vientiane for more options. In addition, dear friends who we had helped come to faith had moved away in their new adventures with Him. We loved teaching at the English Centre yet our initial goal of helping to get it established had been accomplished.

How do you say goodbye? Everyone was shocked and saddened by our news. We would teach one more term from January to the end of May 2020, before heading to Singapore for a couple of weeks to be with family and thank churches and supporters for their interest in our family and Laos over the years. We wanted to communicate in-person how valued and fruitful their partnership with us had been. Then to England to prepare for the start of the academic year in September.

I could not help feeling worried that our unstable neighbour would be hungry without us and get himself into mischief with less-forgiving future tenants. I bought an enormous amount of long-life food and rice porridge packets to keep him going for at least a few months. Every time I popped round to his shack, however, he was mysteriously out and everything was locked up. Moreover, we no longer bumped into him roaming the streets which was strange.

For years, we had been discussing with Mei's family in Singapore about meeting in Bangkok and the upcoming Chinese New Year in 2020 seemed a perfect opportunity. Although our remaining time in Laos was short, it was only a weekend and a fantastic opportunity to celebrate an important family time that we had not been involved in for many years.

As the time drew closer to travel to Bangkok, we picked up news of a flu-like disease that had been discovered in China. Mei's family asked us to bring masks and extra for them as they had sold out in Singapore.

As Singaporeans are the most cautious of the species when it comes to world travel and hygiene, we did not take this too seriously. In any case, masks were not available in Laos either. Perhaps they had sold out too.

Although quite a few people were wearing masks in the Bangkok masses, we were not perturbed as Asian people wear masks as a matter of courtesy for all manner of reasons such as air pollution or for even a little cough. We had a lovely couple of days and enjoyed the sights and the copious amounts of food. Little were we to know that COVID-19 would soon wreak havoc on the world, starting in Asia's megacities.

After returning to Laos, we would discover with horror that Bangkok had long been the choice overseas destination for mainland Chinese folk during Lunar New Year. The virus had arrived with millions of tourists. We were astonished at the risk we had strolled into, particularly for Mei's mother. We were very grateful for His mercy in protecting all of us. Little did we know that this off-chance trip would be the last chance to meet our Singaporean family for a very long time.

We wanted to live every day in Laos as if it was our last. It was not long, however, before the threat of COVID rankled the government into closing all schools in March 2020. It was gut-wrenching to think that our final term at the English Centre and for the girls at their school would finish like this.

Teachers in Laos were among the first in the world to find themselves in the novel position of having to teach online. The girls soon had a disheartening pile of worksheets to complete which was thankfully intermingled with some direct online teaching. At the English Centre, we managed to meet most of our students in the nick of time before lockdown to get them set up for online learning. As a private school, we were initially allowed to teach from our own classrooms before having to shut too. In another mad panic, we managed to upgrade to half-decent internet at home on the day that the official lockdown in Laos started. Imagine scores of workmen drilling and hammering away in our home in the midst of COVID fear and pandemonium.

All the problems that the whole world would soon experience with teaching and learning online were encountered in those early days of COVID. As most of our students were in their early teens and classes took place in the evening, most self-respecting parents were sure to have their youngsters at home. With multiple generations living under one roof, it was no easy task for our students to find a quiet place to study. Clucking chickens, bellowing cows, spluttering motorbikes, and incessant hammering filled our virtual classrooms, along with guest appearances from inquisitive neighbours, rampaging toddlers, and snooping grandmas.

'Village scene' by Kaelyn Whetham

In addition, Lao homes seldom had broadband and most folk used low-quota internet data packages on their phones. Everyone made the most of free internet at the office, cafés, and restaurants. While all our students had access to a phone, they were not ideal for formal, interactive study in groups. Video calls gobbled up the data quota of our students within minutes and people would suddenly drop out, sometimes in mid-sentence.

The Lao aversion to 'The Unknown' also played a part in the challenges with students opting out of class rather than run the risk of being late, not being able to hear or understand, classmates seeing their living conditions in the background, or Mum bellowing for them to come to dinner. Mei was close to tears on occasion and it was a huge relief and very rewarding to get most of our lovely students through their online studies. With the easing of lockdown coinciding with the end of term, we were grateful that we were allowed to have final tests and class parties socially distanced together at the English Centre.

Apart from teaching matters, we were to encounter another huge challenge to our sanity. Just before lockdown was announced and online teaching commenced, we noticed that our business visas needed renewing. Having been through the process countless times over the years, we were not too concerned and dispatched our passports as usual to the Vientiane branch of the English Centre for processing.

About a month later, I received a strange voice message in Lao on my phone from our colleague in Vientiane. There was some sort of problem with Keziah's passport and it had been returned. On investigation, we discovered that we had somehow conspired to overlook the overwhelming fact that the passport was full. There were a few spaces left but no full pages needed for the visa sticker. We could have kicked ourselves. How could this have happened?

We found Laos to be a place that exuded compassion and patience in every situation. People were poised to be accommodating and make exceptions. Try as we might, however, there was nothing we could do but to have the passport returned to us and apply for a new British passport. At the same time, the Lao government announced a strict lockdown would begin in a matter of days. The first step was to contact the company in Vientiane that the British Embassy outsourced to for passport applications. We were only given an email and I spent days sending messages and waiting to see if we could apply remotely. Shockingly, there was not a single reply to our increasingly urgent messages. With lockdown imminent and no information, we quickly filled in the forms to courier the documents from Savannakhet to our friend in Vientiane who kindly agreed to take them in-person to the company office.

While trawling through the internet for information, I noticed that the German Embassy also used the same company for their passports and, with commendable efficiency, had helpfully thought to include a contact number on their website. On trying it, the number went straight through to the UK section! Imagine my astonishment when I was asked to bring my application as soon as possible as the office would be shutting indefinitely in two hours due to the threat of COVID. Not so simple if you live seven hours away.

We had no choice but to put Keziah's passport application on hold. Miraculously, our couriered documents had not been dispatched yet and we managed to retrieve them just before they disappeared and got held up somewhere. Hours later, lockdown ensued with everyone ordered to stay home, with all flights cancelled and borders sealed.

The remarkable thing was that Keziah's passport was returned to us with the separate 'Stay Permit' stapled inside which did not run out until later in the year. We had never heard of such a thing and were very grateful to God for this miracle. There was comfort knowing that with this document, Keziah could prove that she was in the country legally. Moreover, the British Embassy could write a letter to the Lao border police asking that we be allowed to exit the country without hindrance or penalty.

Meanwhile, the days and months since the visa had expired had been mounting up. There was an overstay fine to consider with rumours suggesting $2 to $10 a day depending on which social media post you chanced upon. Was it possible to march confidently through immigration with a valid stay permit but expired visa? Could He make seeing eyes blind? Or soften the hearts of the authorities with compassion in the pandemonium of travel amidst COVID?

Incredibly, the British Embassy's advice was to go to the border police post in Savannakhet and explain ourselves. When I requested an official letter from the Embassy, however, they declined as they deemed the passport full and thus invalid. In other words, we were on our own. Going to immigration without official backing would have been an unthinkably overconfident manoeuvre. Even with a letter, I would have spent the entire day trying to explain my case in Lao to polite yet bewildered policemen. They would have understandably been reluctant to take initiative without permission from higher up. I may have ended up losing a lot of money in fines, had vital documents confiscated, or even ended up being detained myself.

The only other option was to apply for an Emergency Travel Document. To get one, however, the form asked us for our ticket information. How do you book tickets without a valid passport and how do you book flights if there are no flights and borders are closed? This mind-blowing scenario just kept going around in maddening circles. All we could do was place our lives in His hands.

Over the years, we have seen people responding to leaving a place by distancing themselves from situations and people to help soothe the pain of imminent separation. This was completely understandable and preparing to leave was an incredibly busy and stressful time. For us, it was a time that we drew even closer to people. Our hearts were full as people dropped by with an armful of mangoes and other thoughtful gifts such as homemade yoghurt and bread. We cooked sumptuous food for everyone we knew and people insisted on cooking for us too. Our colleagues at the English Centre organised multiple 'thank you' meals at the finest restaurants in town. We hosted fellowships where we prayed and sang our hearts out.

We visited those people in the city we had not seen because of lockdown. We travelled to neighbouring provinces to see cherished friends. We made sure that the children spent lots of time with their friends. It was a joy to even be able to attend an engagement and wedding ceremony of close friends in the countryside. I even managed to help two friends move house, filling my small car with all manner of possessions. It was a hoot saying a prayer while driving past the police checkpoint with fans and mops poking out of the windows.

We had no idea when flights would resume, borders open, or even if we would be allowed to leave the country. Since the terms at the English Centre and the school had finished, it was a great chance to travel to Vientiane and meet all our friends from our many years there. We owed it to them to explain that we would be leaving at some point and how much we valued their presence in our lives. It was a time of great joy sitting down with people as they shared about their lives: a new baby, partner, project, land to build a house on. We noticed with thanksgiving how our friends' daughter who had undergone surgery for a brain haemorrhage was smiling, outgoing, and in good health.

Imagine our shock when on the way home to Savannakhet, we received a call from the passport company to say we had an appointment for Keziah's passport application in two weeks' time. In Vientiane where we had just come from. The thought of having to do the fourteen-hour round trip again so soon was exhausting but there was no choice.

Days later, we travelled to the capital once again to submit the passport application and make the most of the situation to celebrate Keziah's fourteenth birthday with dear friends. On our return to Savannakhet, it was a such a lovely boost for Keziah to meet her best friend who happened to be in town with her family to renew their Thai passports.

An additional worry on the radar was that our house rental for the year was coming to an end in June. My rustic but respectful Lao together with a dose of natural charm persuaded our business-minded but compassionate landlady to accept an extension on a month-by-month basis, a most unusual and kind thing to do. Her decision was one we were very grateful for otherwise we would have had to move to a guesthouse. We still had a houseful of things as we were anything but sure how long we would still need them. We were aiming to leave within the next month but with the volatile situation, were ready to extend for three or six months or even longer. Amidst all of this, we were dealt another blow when we discovered that the school in England that we had applied to for Keziah had no place for her.

From the time of the first lockdown, there were no commercial flights in and out of Laos at all. Only the Koreans had somehow managed to organise chartered flights to Seoul with the next one on 12th August, 2020. Even though it was seven hours the wrong direction to the UK, with a horrendous total journey time, it was the only option.

We were in two minds as there was talk of flights resuming between Laos and Vietnam. We watched helpless, however, as a second COVID wave engulfed Danang in Vietnam and a couple of cases were imported into Vientiane. Immediately, all talk of travel between Laos and Vietnam, or anywhere else for that matter, was dismissed. What the government announcement omitted to clarify, however, was whether these measures included chartered flights. Even with this uncertainty, we decided to go ahead and book the chartered flight to the UK via Seoul. As tickets could only be booked in person in Vientiane, our friend offered to go to the ticket office on our behalf. On arrival, he discovered there were just two horrendously overpriced business class seats left and over twenty people on the waiting list.

Around that time, we heard of a humanitarian flight to Malaysia for diplomats and registered development organisations. As the English Centre where we worked is a business, I had no hope of registering for this flight although it did not prevent me from trying. We also tried the International HQ of our sending organisation but folk there did not know if or how we could register. I decided to ask the UK office to try as they were registered as a charity. After nearly two weeks of trying with very little information, tickets were amazingly booked for 30th August, 2020. This left us only nine days before departure from Vientiane.

That night, we frantically tried to book our onward flights to Manchester as we needed to state up to five countries that we would transit through for Keziah's Emergency Travel Document. As Mei tried to book the tickets, the prices kept doubling and the airline website kept crashing. After the fifth attempt of filling in all the information yet again, we clicked on 'Pay' only for the page to refresh itself without any confirmation. I had to call our UK bank to confirm the payment had been made and after an agonising time of waiting, we received a booking confirmation and I could then apply for the Emergency Travel Passport. I even had to wake Keziah up at 2am in order to take a picture of her for the application. She did so well to remain calm and cheerful.

Our lives were about to get even more complicated as we were requested to attend an 'interview' at the British Embassy for the Emergency Travel Document as Keziah was a minor. We were given hope that we could be exempted because of COVID and because we were so far away from Vientiane meaning risky travel on the crowded overnight bus. Try as we might, however, there was no getting around this interview, no compassion: policies were policies, pandemic or no pandemic. We resigned ourselves to packing up and delivering all manner of household items to friends all over Savannakhet and letting them know we would be leaving very soon to Vientiane.

As the departure day approached, we prepared meals but did not feel like eating a thing. I felt troubled throughout and constantly questioned whether we were doing the right thing. I did not want to leave this place and people. Every morning when I woke up, I wished that all of this had been a dream.

On the morning of our departure, one of my students asked me to meet him for breakfast. As Mei was still busy packing, I thought I would go and have a quick coffee with him before going to buy the bus tickets for that night's travel at 8pm. When I arrived at the café, not one but many of my students from multiple classes over the years had gathered for a very moving send-off breakfast together. In fact, I got so distracted that by the time I arrived at the bus station, there were only four tickets left but with two at the front and two at the back of the bus. Not being seated together only added to the stress!

Our landlady's sister, whom we had just got to know the last month, came over that afternoon to kindly offer us a lift to the bus station. To our dismay, she relayed the shocking news that our neighbour who had caused us no end of trouble had been put in prison. The gossip on the street was that he had been caught stealing. That explained why we had not seen him since August and his house was all locked up when I popped over with food. The news was deeply troubling and we could only commit him to God's mercy in what would undoubtedly be a merciless prison environment.

Almost all our friends, students, and colleagues came to the bus station to see us off. They stood in a circle around us and people of all faiths listened while we were prayed for. When it came to saying goodbye, it felt as if I was betraying and abandoning the people and country we cared so much for. I did not dare stop to think because I knew I could not hold myself together for much longer. We could not hold back the tears as we boarded. In a daze, Kaelyn and I waved from our section at the front of the bus to the mass of wonderful people saying goodbye with all their hearts. Only afterwards did Mei and Keziah explain that there were no windows at their section of the bus and they could not see the sheer love of our friends in that moment.

Although inconvenient, it was a good job that we had left for Vientiane earlier than planned. It took an entire day to finally collect the Emergency Travel Document and a whole morning to get the mandatory COVID tests required before flying. On that Friday afternoon, Mei noticed a new email with our flight booking but for another date. There was no explanation or apology. I stared at the words so long, they started to blur as if they were written in another language.

Dismissing it as a mistake, I immediately called the airline to clarify. Our flight had been cancelled! They had moved us to the next available date. However, COVID restrictions meant we were not allowed to be in the Malaysian airport for more than twenty-four hours. We were forced to cancel and look for another flight. Every time we finished keying in all our details the prices went rocket high. When we tried again after dinner, we managed to click 'Pay' but our bank blocked the payment. After nearly two hours of calling the bank on three different devices, we managed to unblock the payment but by then prices had doubled again! We were left with only one other airline with a very short transit time to Manchester in the UK.

We were off! Once again, we stepped out in faith and obedience, entrusting into God's hands our very identities which were so intertwined with Laos: the people we loved dearly, the satisfaction of helping teachers thrive in English teaching and Lao culture, the English teaching that was so satisfying and vital for the Lao nation, our knowledge of Lao culture and language that we had worked so hard on for many years, the array of contacts and information that had been collected over years, the wonderfully unique and delicious Lao food, and even the Lao weather that enabled a certain way of living that we so appreciated. Our hearts ached and grieved because of our love for all things Lao.

Kaelyn drew three of her very different homes in Laos, England, and Singapore

Our story is a different kind of story because it is a living story that continues. This book is a part of its own story in that the things I have shared will continue to grow and change. I harbour a hope that one day, He will lead us back to Laos to live and work and be with the people we love. For now, we have obeyed His call and are in England, poised and available to follow wherever He calls us.

Years ago, an ugly old tree stump stood in the centre of the garden of a house we rented in Vientiane. Amazingly, over time its spindly branches grew and spread all over the garden, affording shelter from the searing Lao sun. Eventually, glorious yellow flowers emerged from all over the tree, transforming that space with unexpected beauty. The tree resembled our own faltering and error-ridden steps in reaching out to people in Laos, a stump with fledgling and awkward branches, but with the beauty of God bursting through in unexpected circumstances.

Glossary of Lao words in English Script

Transliterating Lao words into English has always been an intriguing and contentious business. There is the French influence which has impacted spelling and pronunciation. There are Chinese and Vietnamese language conventions which vie for influence. Then there is the English language which the Lao have rightly appropriated in unique ways to the Lao context. The result is an endearing flexibility to spelling and pronunciation conventions.

Angkit – England or the UK

Ajaan – teacher

Baci – string-tying ceremony

Bombie – tennis ball-sized munition

Bor – no

Bor ben nyang – it isn't anything / no problem / it doesn't matter

Cow-down – New Year's Eve count down

Doi – ultra polite 'yes' or agreement

Huan hai sao – house for rent

Jao – you / yes

Kha noi – I (literally 'Little Slave')

Falang – foreigner

Khon dang pathet – person from overseas

Jep hua – headache

Khen – reed instrument

Kip – currency of the Lao PDR

Kop jai – thank you

Kor – polite, strong, pleading 'please'

Muan – fun or enjoyment

Nop – greeting with hands pressed together

Pai sai? – Where are you going?

Phi – spirit

Sabaidee – Hello (literally 'Comfortable good?')

Wat – Buddhist temple

Yaba – amphetamines (literally 'crazy drug')

Flowers

Dok champa – frangipani

Dok jia – bougainvillaea

Food

Bing jin – fried kebabs

Bing gai – fried chicken

Khao jee – bread / baguette

Khao niao – sticky rice

Khao biak – thick noodle broth

Khao soy – noodle soup with minced meat and bean paste

Roti – crepe/pancake

Gin som – eat fruit dipped in spices

Ma gin khao – come and eat

Padek – fermented fish sauce

Tam mak hung – papaya salad

Sep – tasty/delicious

Seun sep – Please eat! (literally – 'delicious please!')

Transport

Jumbo – small truck with two rows of seats

Tuk-tuk – auto rickshaw

Sawntaeo – larger, faster version of a tuk-tuk with two rows of seats

Bibliography

Adrianoff, Jean, *Chosen for a Special Joy: The Story of Ted and Ruth Adrianoff* (Chicago: Wingspread Publishers, 2001). Inspiring account of the amazing turning of the Hmong to God in northern Laos.

deBuys, William, *The Last Unicorn: A Search for One of Earth's Rarest Creatures* (Little, Brown and Company. Kindle Edition, 2015). Brilliantly written account of the search for the nearly-extinct *saola* near the mountainous Nakai area of Khammuan province. The descriptions of the habitat are breath-taking.

Dupertois, Silvain, *The Gospel in the Land of a Million Elephants* (Switzerland: La Free, 2013). Moving history of the gospel in Laos, particularly the Swiss Brethren efforts from 1902 which were often sown with many tears.

Evans, Grant, *A Short History of Laos: The Land In Between* (Australia: Allen & Unwin, 2002). Comprehensive, opinionated overview of Laos which could do with an update.

Fucella, Jane, *Behind the Smiles: Tales from Life in Thailand* (Exeter: Onwards and Upwards, 2017). Inspiring account of a family's attempts to make the Good News meaningful to the culture of Thai people including in Isaan province and to Lao folk in Bangkok.

Holt, John Clifford, *Spirits of the Place: Buddhism and Lao Religious Culture* (University of Hawaii Press, 2009). Scholarly and sometimes opinionated account of spirit worship in Laos. The references to Sri Lanka are grating but the focus and detail are very helpful to understanding Lao society.

Kremmer, Christopher, *Stalking the Elephant Kings: In Search of Laos* (Australia: Allen & Unwin, 1997). An account of attempting to get a handle on the lost Lao monarchy, a mysterious and risky endeavour.

Osborne, Milton, *The Mekong: Turbulent Past, Uncertain Future* (New York: Grove Press, 2000). Authoritative, scholarly overview of the region but certain to frustrate all lovers of Laos whenever it inevitably veers away to other nations.

Purgason, Kitty, *Professional Guidelines for Christian English Teachers: How to be a Teacher with Convictions While Respecting Those of Your Students* (California: William Carey Library, 2016). Lots of practical ideas about being confident in the middle ground of living out your faith as a teacher with integrity.

Smith, David I., *On Christian Teaching: Practicing Faith in the Classroom* (Michigan: Eerdmans, 2018). One of the best books to date on faith and teaching. Insightful and practical ideas on how faith impacts pedagogy.

Smith, David and Barbara Carvill, *The Gift of the Stranger: Faith, Hospitality, and Foreign Language Learning* (Michigan: Eerdmans, 2000). Useful insights on the links between teaching, hospitality, and witness.

Snow, Donald, B., *English Teaching as Christian Mission: An Applied Theology* (Scotdale, PA: Herald Press, 2001). Thoughtful and provocative. Essential reading for all Christian English teachers.

Recommended Reading on All Things Laos

de Neui, Paul H. ed., *Seeking the Unseen: Spiritual Realities in the Buddhist World* (Pasadena: William Carey Library, 2016). Intriguing papers on 'power encounters' including a north-east Thailand context similar to Laos.

de Neui, Paul H. ed., *Communicating Christ Through Story and Song: Orality in Buddhist Contexts* (Pasadena: William Carey Library, 2008). A challenge to how our understanding of and approach to words has an impact on sharing our faith.

Fadima, Anne, *The Spirit Catches You and You Fall Down: A Hmong Child, Her American Doctors, and the Collision of Two Cultures* (New York: Farrer, Straus & Giroux, 1997). Remarkably researched and heart-rending account of the interaction between Hmong and American worldviews, spirituality, and epilepsy.

Kounthapanya, Khamphone, *History of the Lao Evangelical Church* (Unpublished paper, 1993). Must-read overview from the late leader of the LEC in Laos.

Murphy, Dervla, *One Foot in Laos* (London: Eland Publishing, 2016). Opinionated and sometimes foolish attempts by an Irishwoman to explore Laos by bicycle and on foot.

Oppel, Lloyd, *Eye of the Tempest* (Thailand: Tonsivit Publishers, 2016). Gripping account of two young men serving God in southern Laos amidst turmoil and war.

Smith, Alex, *A Christian's Pocket Guide to Buddhism* (Scotland: OMF/Christian Focus Publications, 2009). Essential reading for anyone interested in connecting with Buddhist people.

Smithies, Michael, *Village Vignettes* (Bangkok: Orchid Press, 2003). Humorous and irreverent take on everyday village life in a north-east Thailand environment often resembling Laos.

Watson, Rosemary, *As the Rock Flower Blooms* (OMF Singapore, 1984). One of the first accounts of Christian outreach in the south of Laos.

Yang, Kao Kalia, *The Latehomecomer: A Hmong Family Memoir* (Bangkok: Orchid Press, 2003). Stirring account of a family forced to flee the terror of war in Laos.